A Paradiso Year

Autumn & Winter Cooking

DENIS COTTER

PHOTOGRAPHY BY JÖRG KÖSTER

DESIGN AND ART DIRECTION BY JOHN FOLEY

First published in 2005 by

Atrium

(an imprint of Cork University Press)

Youngline Industrial Estate

Pouladuff Road

Togher

Cork

Ireland

© Denis Cotter 2005

Photographs © Jörg Köster 2002–2003

Designed by John Foley at Bite, Cork
Set in Adobe Minion

Repro by The Scanning Shop, Dublin

Printed in Great Britain by Butler & Tanner.

British Library Cataloguing in Publication data
A CIP catalogue record for this book is available from the British Library.

Denis Cotter has asserted his moral right, under the Copyright and Related Rights Act 2000, in this work.

ISBN 0-9535353-7-1
A CIP record for this publication is available from the Library of Congress.

For all Atrium books visit www.corkuniversitypress.com

Visit Café Paradiso on the internet at www.cafeparadiso.ie

Introduction

I know some people who hate the coming of autumn. You may know some yourself. For all I know you could be one. You may well be reading this under a pile of crumpled blankets, fuming at the shortening days. My favourite vegetable grower is one. Maybe all growers are. I haven't checked, but now that I think of it, they do get grumpy this time of year. For them, autumn signals the end of growth and the irreversible beginning of decay. Golden leaves twirling gently from the trees have no beauty nor will they become part of future nostalgia. No, the leaves are dead and their persistent tumbling is only flaunting the oncoming decay in an infuriating way that is almost taken personally. Every year, when the summer harvest is at its peak, like children in the sand dunes, they cling to the hope that it will go on longer this year; that the tomato plants won't droop, that the green beans will go on producing crops forever and that there will still be strawberries tomorrow morning. Every year, the same cycle disappoints and infuriates them.

Well, I like autumn. And, like many city dwellers who don't garden, I love the cooling days and the changing colours of leaves. Last autumn, I spent a week in Sweden, where the forests are incredibly beautiful at this time of year, with their random, natural mix of evergreens and deciduous trees. I will, however, grant that you need a long hot summer to appreciate autumn. Even the most determinedly indoors-inclined of us will resent the oncoming of cool days after a 'summer' of them. Autumn is the time to forget the frivolous pleasures of the beach, and turn your mind again to the downtown pleasures of film, jazz, warm pubs, and indoor dinners with hot food and red wine.

But then, I am a consumer, not a producer, and some of my favourite vegetables come along in the next few months. Oh, for sure, its hard to let go of the wonderful foods of summer, when the cooking is light and simple, bursting with sweetness and intense herbs. But, you know, there is a downside to all that bounty too. At least, there is if you are a professional cook trying to use everything that someone else is growing for you. Summer food is impatient. It wants to be picked, now, now, now. And eaten today, not left to become droopy and sad. Green beans and sugar snaps on the vine will be too big and tough tomorrow, tomatoes will literally burst, courgettes will be marrows. Pick it, cook it, eat it, hurry, hurry. It can be such a difficult juggling act to carry off, balancing the quantities that a farmer grows with those that a cook can convince his customers to buy and eat. Especially if the farmer is almost obsessively devoted to his plants and needs to know that their crop is all gone to a good use.

Then autumn arrives with its solid crops of vegetables, and the pressure drops. Is there anything more solid than a pumpkin? Especially the New Zealand Crown variety, which Ultan grows for us and which will store well into winter. Just as spring has a dramatic effect on our cooking after the heaviness of winter, autumn reins it in again, slows it down. As much as I love summer produce, the cook in me welcomes the chance to put away the salad tongs and get out some serious pots and pans. Buy some cream, even. Do a little reducing! Pumpkins and leeks are the bedrock of my cooking in autumn. Both carry rich flavours well, they can cope with long cooking, spices, strong cheeses and the hardier herbs like rosemary and thyme. These two have become synonymous with autumn for me. They are perfectly of their time, in that way that nature has of giving us food that is so appropriate to its time of year.

This is equally true in winter when the available produce is dominated by hardy greens and the many edible roots: carrots, turnips, parsnips and celeriac predominantly. These are foods that are perfect for dishes we love, need even, to eat in the cold dark days. Stews, soups, rich bakes and roasts, slow braises.

It would be pushing the bounds of faith to expect anyone to believe that you might look forward to winter. Winter is something we put up with. It puts the rest of the seasons in context, reminds us how gentle and productive they are. And, yes, we can knock some fun out of it, but we don't look forward to it. When I was working on *Paradiso Seasons*, the plan was to write, photograph and design the book almost simultaneously, so that it would be created through the seasons that it was presenting. In mid-autumn, long before the first frost, the amount of material was running way over the size and budget planned for. I made a more-than-half-serious proposal that we end the book a couple of recipes into winter, leaving the readers with the suggestion that they either emigrate to the other hemisphere or hibernate. I just didn't fancy tackling winter with its roots and cupboard ingredients. How the hell can you amuse people with roots? And yet, when we got down into it, I think it was one of the most inventive periods – writing by the fireplace in almost non-existent afternoons, the kitchen piled with roots, spuds and cabbages, the cupboard full of tins and packets of dry goods. You have to be in winter to appreciate it, and you have to be left with only winter foods to love them, and to make good food from them for the ones you love. This is the essence of seasonal cooking. Working with the foods of the season because they are your best chance of making really pleasureable food at that moment.

Its not always easy to even grasp the notion of the seasonality of food, especially if you shop in supermarkets. It seems to be a great fear of these outlets that if they don't have a large quantity of every product on their shelves every day of the year, that you will go somewhere else to get it. The increasing truth is that you have become so bored with eating poor out-of-season, mass-produced, flown-across-the-hemispheres imitations of asparagus, peaches, melons and beans that you are already going elsewhere. You are looking to buy real food from the man who grew it, or the man whom you trust and who knows the man who grew it. There is a growing disillusionment with the cheap, plentiful but dull food that has been the result of the mass-production systems of the second half of the twentieth century. Well-intended as the drive for cheap food was, it tore apart our relationship with food and left us feeling alienated and unable to satisfy our complex appetites. It is telling that the renewed interest in buying from producers at markets is being driven by consumers need to make contact, as much as by producers need to find a market. The need to repair our relationship with food is also part of the motivation behind the Slow Food Movement. Yet, the Movement's guiding principle is to strive to restore the right to pleasure in food, realising that real pleasure cannot be had in a damaged relationship.

All of these shifts in the food culture are inter-locked and working in the same direction. We want to understand our food, and to know that it has a time and a place, perhaps even a face. In essence, we want to reclaim the rich and complex, but ultimately simple, pleasure of eating well.

As always, I hope that the recipes in this book help you to cook well but, equally, I hope that they encourage you to shop well.

About the recipes

This is not intended to be a comprehensive collection of recipes. I haven't gathered up all the recipes I could think of for every vegetable I could identify. There are many books, written by more knowledgeable people, that are far closer to being authoritative manuals of vegetable cooking, of which two of my favourites are Alice Waters' *Chez Panisse Vegetables* and Digby Law's *A Vegetable Cookbook*. Instead, I have tried to use a small number of recipes to give a sense of the variety of dishes and styles that each vegetable can be used in. The vegetables are most, but not all, of my favourites over the course of a year. There are one or two vegetables missing that I simply didn't use much of in that particular year. It happens. Some years, some vegetables just drift by outside my focus. And some years, crops of vegetables are bountiful and beautiful; next year, it's a washout.

The recipes of each primary vegetable are grouped together, and the vegetables are arranged in a seasonal order, flowing through the year. 'Order' may be the wrong word here. The book was written through one year of seasons, and the layout derives from the order in which the vegetables came to me. Some vegetables have very long seasons, others flit by like butterflies. In my interpretations of the seasons, I buy produce primarily from local growers, but supplement and stretch the seasons with produce from other parts of the country and Europe. Hence, broad beans appear in the book in spring, when I first get them from a French organic grower, even though in a bad year the pods won't show a bulge in Ireland until mid summer. Black kale finds itself slotted into early summer, although research suggests it is naturally a vegetable of early winter in north Italy. However, my first grateful sighting of it each year is much earlier, and it is far too beautiful to be turned away.

If we were to do the same book in another year, rest assured the vegetables would, by their own or their growers single-minded stubbornness, show up in a slightly different order. I like this. It is much more stimulating to be reacting to the availability of produce than to be writing menus first and phoning in orders to make them happen.

Besides, I wanted the flow of the book to reflect the reality of seasonal changes. I've never been comfortable with the neat compartmentalisation of the year into four even-sized seasons. I sometimes argue that there are probably seven, but when I tried to tie the recipes to these, they still didn't fit. It's not really possible, but often done, to put a menu together at the start of each of the four official seasons using ingredients that are all present at the start and end of the 'season'. In spring, you would have no asparagus at the start and no sprouting broccoli at the end; in summer there would be no peppers, peaches or beans until halfway through or later. The reality is that vegetables are unaware of our breakdown of the year and show up in their own good time and in a raggle-taggle order. In Café Paradiso, I like to think that there has only ever been one menu. Rather than throwing it out at the end of August, for example, to be replaced by the 'Autumn' menu, that one menu responds to the ebb and flow of the vegetables through the year. They come and go one or two at a time, and the menu follows suit, changing a little here and there every now and again.

While some of the recipes in this collection are frequent features of the Café Paradiso menu, and are complex and conscious of their appearance, as restaurant food must be, most were devised at home and are intended for regular home use.

Some are little more than simple ways to prepare vegetables, and these are obviously open to personal interpretation. They can be simple dinners, side dishes or the starting point for something more elaborate. The recipes are always about the primary vegetable, and if a recipe pairs a vegetable with a spice or a cheese, chances are those two will be good together in any context. Take what you want from the recipes. I hope they are useful as reference points as much as definite instructions.

Don't undermine your precious vegetables with poor support. You should be just as fussy about your oils, vinegars, cheeses, flours, grains and so on. Unless something else is specified in a recipe, 'olive oil' always means a good extra virgin one; 'balsamic vinegar' means a traditionally aged one from Modena, at least five years old; 'butter' means nothing less than real butter, and do try to use Irish butter – it has a richness of flavour I've never come across anywhere else.

Although this may seem a little uptight, many of the recipes give very specific instructions on chopping and slicing vegetables. This is not just for appearances; how the vegetable is cut affects how it cooks as well as the final texture and character of the dish. Two of the greatest sins in vegetable cooking are using random combinations of 'mixed veg' and careless cutting. Don't always cut a vegetable the same way: the thin diagonal slice of carrot used in a stirfry will obviously be hopeless for roasting. You don't always have to follow my cutting methods exactly; but when you approach a vegetable with a knife, stop for a second or two to think about the final dish. Try to get a clear sense of what you want to end up with, and then decide how to cut the vegetable to suit the dish.

Finally, all quantities in the recipes are net values; that is after all peeling and trimming – the amount, in other words, that you are putting in the pan.

Happy cooking.

Autumn

blueberries

blackberries

mushrooms

aubergines

figs

pumpkins

leeks

Lemon verbena, ricotta and white chocolate pudding with blueberry compote

Blueberries are a mystery to me; bland and uninteresting raw, they make great jam and sauces and are wonderful in pancakes, tarts and cheesecakes. This pudding is as good or better, depending on your preference, with a compote of summer berries – the red, white and black currants that birds pinch from our garden before we get even a cupful – or with blackberries or raspberries. The recipe is actually all about the lemon verbena, a bush that grows at the back door of our house to mask the smell of our ageing dog, Paddy. The bush has an astonishing smell, part zest of citrus and part sherbet. Waving it in someone's face unfailingly gets an amazed reaction. I don't remember where the bush came from, but the dictionary says it is South American with sedative qualities! If that smell can put you to sleep, you're already dead. The shrub grows to about five feet high over the summer, then I gradually reduce it to a skeleton and next year it does it all again. God, I love that plant, though it may well be wishing that I would leave it to grow into a tree. Given all of that, it's amazing how many leaves it takes to flavour a custard. I suspect it's all volatile scent that's easily lost. When I tried reducing the quantity of leaves in this recipe, the pudding lost its flavour. The syrup holds the flavour better. It's unlikely that you'll find lemon verbena to buy, so all I can do is encourage you to plant it. If you never make a pudding, you will come to love the scent by your back door.

FOR SIX PUDDINGS:

150mls cream
30 lemon verbena leaves
300g white chocolate
200g ricotta
3 eggs
3 egg whites

350g caster sugar
300g blueberries

Warm the cream, without boiling, and pour it over 20 of the lemon verbena leaves in a bowl. Leave this to infuse until the cream has cooled.

Melt the chocolate in a bowl over hot water and leave it to cool a little.
Put the ricotta in a food mixer with the infused cream and beat them gently to soften the cheese. Add the eggs and egg whites and beat again to incorporate them. Fold in the chocolate.

Heat an oven to 180°c/350°f. Butter six small pudding moulds of 150mls capacity and place a circle of baking parchment in the base of each. Fill the moulds with the pudding custard and place them in an oven dish. Pour boiling water into the oven dish to come halfway up the moulds, and place the dish in the oven, to cook for one and a half hours. The puddings should be just set, not too firm or baked. It may take a little longer. Leave the puddings in their moulds for at least ten minutes, and in any case until you need them. They should be served warm or at room temperature.

While the puddings are cooking, make a syrup by putting 100g sugar in a pan with 100mls water and bringing it slowly to a boil. Drop in the remaining lemon verbena leaves and simmer for three minutes until you have a slightly thickened syrup.

Put 250g sugar in a small pan with the blueberries and a tablespoon of water. Bring this very slowly to a boil and simmer for five minutes until the fruit is soft.

Place the puddings on plates, discarding the parchment paper, and spoon a teaspoon of the lemon verbena syrup over each one, maybe a few drops more. Place some berries in their juices around each pudding.

Blackberry tart with Calvados ice cream

As the year turns and foods come back around into season, I try to look equally hard at the old standard recipes and new ways to work with them. I never do that with blackberries. For anyone over a certain age, the mere mention of blackberry picking is an instant key to a kaleidoscope of memories, triggering images, emotional throw-backs, longings and nostalgia. I could lead you, blindfold, from any point on the planet to the field where my strongest blackberry memories were formed. I recently heard a radio presenter holding forth about people buying blackberries in super-markets instead of picking them from the hedgerows themselves. There's something in that; perhaps people are too busy going to garden centres and DIY stores on Sunday afternoons to notice the blackberries. But it is even more true that there are not so many hedges, brambles or blackberries to be found, and you practically need government clearance to walk on farmland. Where are we to pick our blackberries? The hedges in our small garden (and the neighbours' gardens too) in Cork city have a few brambles scattered through them. We scrounge a few blackberries every day during the season, enough to make a tart only by many days of steely-minded absti-nence from casual picking – it doesn't happen every year! For the blackberries in the tart photographed here and the plate it was baked on, I have to thank my neighbour Mrs Mary Gamble, who picked the fruit on a long damp Sunday afternoon walk.

If you have a regular supply of blackberries, you'll have your own favourite recipes, probably including one for a tart you're very fond of. I hope you also eat huge bowls of berries tossed in sugar with a blob of cream on top, and that in good years you make jam. Which means, I suppose, that this recipe is actually for those of you who don't usually make blackberry tart, which must mean those of you who don't pick blackberries. Hey, get out there and pick blackberries!! It's going to be winter soon.

Calvados is an apple brandy traditionally made in Normandy in the north of France – blackberries and apples… that's as ancient and perfect as it gets.

FOR THE ICE CREAM:
1 cinnamon stick
300mls milk
5 egg yolks
125g caster sugar
300mls cream
2 tablespoons Calvados liqueur

Break the cinnamon stick and put it in a pan with the milk. Heat the milk to just short of boiling for one minute.

Whisk the egg yolks and sugar together until they are thick and pale. Still whisking, on low speed, pour in the milk through a sieve. Return this egg and milk custard to the pan and simmer, stirring all the time, until it is thick enough to coat the back of a spoon. Leave the custard to cool before adding the cream and the Calvados. Freeze using an ice cream machine.

FOR THE TART:

120g unsalted butter
240g plain flour
40g caster sugar
1 egg
1 tablespoon cornflour
500g blackberries
150g caster sugar
1 egg, beaten

Rub the butter into the flour, using your fingers or short bursts in a food processor. Transfer this to a bowl and stir in the sugar. Beat the egg lightly and add enough cold water to give 60mls of liquid. Stir this into the flour with a few quick strokes of a wooden spoon, then knead very briefly to get a smooth dough. Divide the dough into two flattened balls and chill them for an hour or more.

Heat an oven to 190°C/375°F. Roll one pastry ball to line a tart tin of 26cm diameter and 3cm high, leaving the pastry hanging a little over the edge. Sprinkle the cornflour over, through a sieve. Pile in the blackberries and sprinkle over the sugar. Roll out the second pastry ball to a diameter a few centimetres wider than the tart case. Brush the rim of the lower pastry with water. Use a rolling pin to pick up the second pastry and place it over the tart carefully. Press the edges together

and trim off the excess pastry. Press the rim of the pastry with a fork or the flat side of a knife to strengthen the seal. Brush the top of the pastry with beaten egg and make a couple of cuts in the top. Bake in the oven for 30 minutes until the pastry is browned and crisp, and the blackberry juices are bubbling up through the cuts. Leave the tart to cool for at least ten minutes, and serve it warm or at room temperature with the Calvados ice cream or simply a dollop of cream.

Field mushrooms in milk with herbs and garlic

I'm not really a mushroom lover. They simply don't get me excited the way fresh green produce does. Woodland mushrooms taste too much of the dark, dank places they grow in for my liking; though I make an exception for truffles, which I adore. Still, this embarrasses me a little sometimes, professionally speaking, because mushrooms are so much a part of restaurant culture, especially exotic and wild mushrooms.

Vegetarians in a restaurant are as likely to be offered 'wild' mushrooms as the ubiquitous goats' cheese, because they are perceived to be high-value items, something exotic you might not have at home. The restaurant trade is full of such profitable gems.

Confusingly, I can also claim to really like the taste of mushrooms – cultivated mushrooms, that is. Mushroom cultivation is an industry often derided, usually rightly, for churning out cheap, flavourless and chemically produced fodder. But there are exceptions. I love the oyster mushrooms we get from Forest Mushrooms in North Cork, for their delicate, elegant flavour. I like the dark-skinned organically cultivated 'chestnuts', or 'Paris browns' and their bigger cousins, the portobello; and I even like your standard cultivated supermarket mushroom when it's a little oversized with open gills, and fried in lots of garlic butter. I'm aware that what I like about these mushrooms is that their flavour is similar, though inferior, to that of the rarest mushroom of all, and my favourite by a long way, the 'common' field mushroom. Neither sophisticated, exotic nor expensive, and now no longer even common, it has changed in my lifetime from an abundant seasonal treat to a very rare one. This seems to be a consequence of modern farming methods, which have simply left nowhere for the mushroom to live. If you do find 'field mushrooms' on restaurant menus, do ask if they are from a field known to the cook or if they are simply large, open commercial mushrooms that have never seen a field. If the cook has indeed found the mushrooms in a field, it's unlikely he'll tell you where it is.

Those of you lucky enough to have access to field mushrooms in late summer/early autumn will have your own favourite way to eat them, but you might like to try this. Anyone else curious enough to try it might find that it works reasonably well with commercial mushrooms with open gills.

The essence of this dish is how my mother cooked mushrooms when I was a child. We knew of only one mushroom, the field mushroom, which popped up in late August and September in the fields left fallow between crops or used only for casual cattle grazing or hay harvesting. We cooked them in two ways – fried in butter or boiled in milk. This recipe involves a bit of meddling with the classic, which had neither herbs nor garlic. It is so simple that I'm still a little embarrassed to be writing it down, but I promise that it is divine to eat. Serve with buttered crusty bread.

FOR FOUR:

400g field mushrooms
1 litre milk
4 cloves garlic, sliced
small handful chopped herbs (one or more of parsley, thyme and lovage)
1 tablespoon chopped chives
salt and black pepper, to season

Break the large mushrooms into halves or quarters, leave the smaller ones whole. Put them in a pan with the milk, garlic and herbs, bring it to a boil and simmer for 15 to 20 minutes until the mushrooms are tender and the milk has taken on a light chocolate colour. Stir in the chives. Share out the mushrooms into shallow bowls, ladle the broth over them and season with lots of salt and coarsely ground black pepper.

Baked portobello mushroom with Cashel blue cheese, pecan crumbs and sage, and smoked paprika aioli

One of these mushrooms can make a substantial first course, and sometimes a main course. Portobellos come in very impressive sizes, and have an impressively weighty feel in the hand. When baked, as in this recipe, they become deliciously juicy, and the flavour and smell are intensely, well, mushroomy. They need to be, because there are a lot of flavours in this dish; all flavours that go very well with mushrooms in their own right, so it's simply a matter of balance – avoid any one being too dominant and you will get a blend that still lets the mushroom shine through.

Sage butter is my favourite way to use the herb, and there is always a jug of it in the Paradiso fridge. Cashel blue cheese is a firm, though not dry, cheese from Tipperary, and the piece I use here is from a matured round. Because there is so little cheese on each mushroom, using a mild or young 'blue' cheese will not have sufficient effect. Buy the cheese, and any cheese for that matter, from a cheese shop where you can see, and taste, what you are buying. A Gorgonzola or similar would be very good here too.

Smoked paprika should taste of the peppers it was made from, with quite heavy smoky undertones. At the moment, I have two varieties, both Spanish: one is sweet, made from sweet peppers, and the other is hot, made from hot peppers. Both are defiantly as they advertise themselves, and, rather than choose between them, I mix them for a wonderful blend that gives a smoky, sweet flavour but with a respectable kick of heat too. Amazing stuff. Spanish paprika is the best I've come across, though I'm sure there are Hungarians and Turks who would argue that one with you. If you make this aioli with cheap paprika, 'produce of more than one country', you will get nothing more than a lovely red emulsion. I have listed lemon juice as an ingredient in the aioli, but I don't always use it – remember this is not a mayonnaise, and how acid, or not, you want it to be is totally up to you, and what you're eating it with. Taste the aioli and decide if you would like a few drops of lemon in it; try that and think about more – let your own tastebuds decide.

FOR FOUR:

4 cloves garlic

1 egg

1 egg yolk

1 teaspoon Dijon mustard or similar

250mls olive oil

1 teaspoon smoked paprika

salt and pepper, to season

juice of half a lemon

450g butter

1 bunch sage leaves

30g pecans

30g day-old bread

4 large portobello mushrooms

50g mature Cashel blue cheese, or similar

First make the aioli. Cut the ends off the garlic cloves and roast the cloves in a low to medium oven until the garlic is soft, then squeeze the garlic from its skin. Put the garlic in a food processor with the egg, egg yolk and mustard, and blend for one minute. Pour in the olive oil in a slow stream until the aioli thickens, then add the paprika and some salt and pepper. Taste it, and add some lemon juice to your own taste. Clarify the butter to remove the milk solids. Put it back in a clean pan with most of the sage leaves, leaving a few, and bring it to a boil. Leave this to cool and for the butter to absorb the sage flavour. Put the pecans in a food processor with the bread and process to get a breadcrumb texture. Spread this on an oven tray and toast it in a medium oven until crisp, tossing occasionally to ensure even cooking. When it is crisp, put it in a bowl, chop the remaining sage leaves and stir them in.

Brush the mushrooms with the sage butter, sprinkle with a little salt and bake them in a moderate oven for eight to ten minutes until they are tender – check by piercing them with a knife. Crumble some cheese over each, sprinkle on some of the pecan crumbs, and put the mushrooms back in the oven for a few minutes more until the cheese begins to melt. Serve one mushroom each with some smoked paprika aioli.

Oyster mushroom ravioli with a truffled lovage cream and peas

The filling in these ravioli is a very simple one because I want it to taste of the delicate flavour of the oyster mushrooms and it needs to be simple to live with the richly flavoured sauce. Lovage isn't a very widely available herb, which is surprising given its exciting flavour and the fact that it grows easily in bushes of long stems with large wide leaves. In appearance it is a bit like a celery plant gone wild, and that's a fairly good description of its flavour too: it's celery, but it's more than celery – celery exaggerated, celery from *Alice in Wonderland*. Perhaps if it were a little more timid it would be more popular. It is fantastic with potatoes and eggs; it can turn a stodgy comfort soup into something refreshing and lively, and is a delightful flavour to come across in a salad of mixed greens. Always add lovage at the very end of cooking, to preserve its exuberant qualities.

I use truffle oil to add a tiny high note to the lovage cream, a hint or suggestion of another flavour. Be very careful not to use it to drown the flavours of the dish. Truffle oil, as it is available in shops, is usually a light oil such as sunflower that has been flavoured with essence of white truffles. Disdained by those who have access to, and the wallets for, real white truffles of Alba, white truffle oil is a remarkably good product, and an incredibly cheap one given how few drops it takes to flavour a meal. It can be lethal in the hands of a heavy-handed chef desperate to add value to your expensive dinner. The flavour is so heady it is almost more scent than taste; it will certainly be the first thing you smell in a dish, but it shouldn't be the only thing you taste; I like it best when it is so elusive that it is a mere suggestion of a scent floating in the heavy air above your plate. Go easy with that bottle, boys and girls. While it may originally have been a whimsy to put the slightly unseasonal peas in the dish, I love the fresh contrast they bring to it.

FOR FOUR STARTERS:

1 tablespoon butter

150g oyster mushrooms, chopped finely

2 cloves garlic, chopped finely

1 tablespoon white wine

salt and pepper, to season

2 tablespoons very fine breadcrumbs

2 sheets fresh pasta, approx 16cm x 60cm

150mls light stock (see page 137)

150mls white wine

400mls cream

salt and pepper, to season

4–6 lovage leaves

white truffle oil

50g peas

Melt the butter in a wide, shallow pan and cook the mushrooms and garlic over high heat for two minutes. Add the wine and cook for one minute more. Remove from the heat immediately, season with salt and pepper, and leave to cool before stirring in the breadcrumbs.

Lay the pasta on a work surface and cut out twenty four circles of eight centimetres in diameter. Take a rounded teaspoonful of the filling. Roll it into a ball and place it in the centre of one of the circles of pasta. Brush the visible part of the pasta circle with water and place one of the larger pieces on top. Now press the edges together firmly while, at the same time, taking care not to leave any air pockets inside the parcel. Repeat this with the rest of the circles – you need three each for a starter, more for a main course.

Bring the stock and wine to a boil in a pan, and simmer until the volume is reduced by half. Add the cream and simmer for a few minutes until the sauce thickens to a nice pasta-coating consistency – try some on the back of a wooden spoon to get an idea. Season carefully with salt and pepper. Keep the sauce warm, or make it before you start to cook the ravioli and reheat it gently. Just before you serve, chop the lovage and add it to the sauce, then shake in a little truffle oil – one or two drops per person is enough.

To cook the pasta, bring a large pot of water to a boil and drop in the ravioli. If you think the parcels might be overcrowded, do two batches. As with all pasta, the only way to decide that it's cooked is to test it, so nick a tiny bit off one of the ravioli and taste it. Remove the ravioli with a slotted spoon and put them in a bowl with a little olive oil to prevent them sticking to each other. If you do two batches, tip the first one back into the pot just as the second batch is cooked and remove the lot in half a minute.

Serve three ravioli per portion with some cream poured over each. Scatter a few lightly cooked peas on each portion.

Pan-fried mushrooms in sage and cider cream with a potato, parsnip and wild rice cake, and beetroot relish

This recipe works with most mushrooms, so use your favourites. I usually make it with mild oyster mushrooms, sometimes mixed with those lovely dark-skinned organic chestnut mushrooms. If your preference is towards wild woodland mushrooms or shiitakes, some of those in a mix would be fine too. Just don't invite me round.

If you have sage butter in your fridge, as in the earlier recipe for portobello mushrooms, use that to fry the mushrooms and you will need fewer or no sage leaves.

It's important to fry the mushrooms over a fairly high heat, so if you have doubts about the capacity of your pan or cooker elements, fry the mushrooms in two batches, then return them to the pan before adding the cider.

The potato cakes came about during one of my occasional attempts to find a rosti recipe that would work consistently in the restaurant without driving me crazy every second or third time I used it. It's a personal weakness I come back to every now and again, then walk away from, telling myself it really doesn't matter, life's too short, etc etc. Eventually I decided to limit myself to trying to make a potato and parsnip cake recipe that didn't need eggs to stand up, but wasn't just sculptured mash. This is it, and I'm not going back to rosti again. The texture of the cooked potatoes is important: use a medium floury potato such as a rooster, which will hold its shape but has some starch; chop the cooked potatoes with a knife to get a 'coarse mash' – that is, a mixture of various-sized lumps of potato. There is no scientific way to achieve this better than randomly chopping with a knife. The cakes are flavoured with fresh thyme and rosemary oil. The oil in the cake mix will help the insides of the cakes to cook rather than simply heat through. However, if you don't make the rosemary oil, use plain olive oil and another herb such as parsley, chives or lovage, as raw rosemary can be too overpowering.

This is a very rich meal, so I would add some fresh greens for light relief. It's a personal thing, and you may prefer your rich, creamy dishes uncompromised. If you are of my tendency, you could serve a separate side dish of cooked green beans or broccoli, but my favourite is to wilt some greens – kale, spinach or cabbage – in olive oil and water, and to serve a little pile under each potato cake.

The beetroot relish is sweet, with the distinctive taste of caraway, so use just a little blob for each portion. The recipe is for more than you will need but it will keep well for a week or two.

FOR FOUR:

olive oil

500g beetroot, washed and grated

500g red onions, halved and thinly sliced

1 tablespoon caraway seeds

half teaspoon nutmeg

100mls balsamic vinegar

100g brown sugar

large pinch cayenne pepper

a little salt

100g wild rice

500g rooster potatoes, or similar, peeled and quartered

200g parsnips, peeled and grated

2 sprigs fresh thyme

2 tablespoons rosemary oil

salt and pepper, to season

400g mushrooms

4 tablespoons butter

4 cloves garlic, chopped

8 sage leaves

150mls dry cider

300mls cream

Heat some olive oil in a pan and put in the beets, onions, caraway seeds and nutmeg. Cook, stirring often, until the onions are soft, then add the balsamic vinegar and sugar, and simmer for at least 20 minutes, until the vegetables are very soft and the liquid has become thick and syrupy. Season with the cayenne pepper and a little salt. Leave to cool.

Cook the wild rice at a simmer in boiling water until it has softened, about 40 minutes, then drain it. Steam the potatoes until just done, then chop them into a coarse mash. Add the parsnips to the potato with the wild rice, thyme, rosemary oil and some salt and pepper. Stir gently to combine everything without breaking the potato any more. Place four metal rings, 9cm in diameter and 3cm high, in a wide frying pan. Brush them and the pan with oil and set it over a low heat. Pack the rings with the cake mix to begin cooking gently. After about five minutes, flip the cakes to cook on the other side. You may need to flip them a few more times, and to shuffle the cakes around the pan, to cook them evenly. They should cook all the way through, and become crisp and lightly browned on the outsides.

While the cakes are cooking, slice or tear any large mushrooms in half, leaving the small ones whole. Melt the butter in a wide pan, turn the heat to high and toss in the mushrooms and garlic. Cook, stirring, over high heat, until the mushrooms begin to colour, adding more butter if they seem too dry. Slice the sage leaves, add them to the pan with the cider and boil it on high for two minutes, then pour in the cream. Bring it back to a boil and simmer for one minute. Serve immediately.

Aubergine, tomato and goats' cheese galette with a balsamic-tomato emulsion

This was one of my first aubergine dishes, and one that I am very fond of, but in thought more than use. I gave it up for a long time because, as the restaurant got busier and busier, it became a nightmare to produce in large volumes night after night. John Healy, who was cooking with me in Paradiso at the time, became very fond of the dish, in his perverse way, and he would cook it for me occasionally when he invited us round to his lovely home for dinner. What a treat that was, to have John Healy cook dinner for you. I miss him, but he's in Auckland now, gardening and studying the fine art of jewellery. If you come across him, try to wangle an invitation to dinner. I recently rediscovered the dish when I cooked at home for some friends, and it was a lovely meal to prepare. I think the scale of four portions suits it, maybe six at most; any more and there will be some gnashing of teeth and a fine old mess.

The galettes are very simple constructions of very compatible ingredients, and the success of the dish depends on careful preparation. Slice the tomatoes and cheese as thinly as you can, construct the layers neatly and evenly, and, above all, remember that the finished galettes need only be warmed through, not baked. Too long in the oven and the cheese will run off, and the whole balance of the dish will be lost. Balance is the key – no one ingredient should dominate, especially not the cheese.

The balsamic emulsion, as with all dishes using balsamic vinegar, needs a good vinegar – a very good vinegar, in fact: it needs the fruitiness and the rich, concentrated sweetness as much as it needs acidity. It also needs a good strong blender. If your sauce separates after a while, simply blend or whisk it back together just before you use it. Serve some lightly cooked greens to balance the richness of the galettes. It should store fine in the fridge for a week or so.

FOR FOUR:

4 aubergines
olive oil, to coat
4–6 large tomatoes
300g goats' cheese, from a large log
4 tablespoons olive tapenade or use a shop-bought one
1 bunch basil leaves
black pepper, to season

1 clove garlic
200mls olive oil
80mls tomato passata
60mls balsamic vinegar
salt and pepper, to season

Shave a slice off two long sides of each aubergine, then lay the aubergines on a cut side and slice them horizontally into four flat slices from each aubergine. Brush the slices lightly with olive oil and roast them in a hot oven, about 190°C/375°F until lightly coloured, but fully cooked. Slice the tomatoes very thinly and discard the seeds. Slice the cheese very thinly too – it may help to have it very well chilled before you attempt this. If the cheese does fall apart, don't worry – you can use it in a patchwork way just as well as in neat slices.

Choose sets of four well-matched slices of aubergine, or better still reunite the original aubergines. Set aside the best-looking ones to be the top slices. Spread a thin layer of tapenade on each of the bottom slices, then cover this with a layer of tomato slices, then cheese slices, then torn basil leaves. Season with black pepper but no salt. Place another slice of aubergine on top, press it gently and repeat the tomato, cheese and basil layers. Put on another slice of aubergine and repeat the process. Finally put the top slices on and press gently.

When you are ready to serve the galettes, place them on an oven tray lined with baking parchment, and bake them in the oven at 160°C/325°F for 15 to 20 minutes. Remember that you are just trying to warm the galettes rather than bake them. They are done when the cheese has softened but has not quite started to run.

While the galettes are warming, make the sauce. Crush the garlic and put it in a jug with the rest of the ingredients. Use a hand blender to blend everything to a thick emulsion, then season it well with plenty of black pepper and a little salt.

Serve one galette per person, with a thin stream of balsamic emulsion poured around each.

Fresh linguine with aubergine-tomato relish

More often than not, aubergines with pasta suggests to me roasted slices of aubergine tossed with a dried pasta like penne or rigatoni in olive oil with, say, chillies, garlic, basil if I've got it, leeks maybe, and some fresh greens such as rocket, spinach or kale. Occasionally, and this is a very private thing, I like to use this rich aubergine relish as a sauce for fresh pasta. Private, in that the relish is rarely used for pasta in Paradiso except by me. I like to take a little from the fridge on a Sunday evening to make a pasta sauce at home. As you can tell by the spicing, the relish has roots in both eastern and western cooking, and can easily be adapted to either. I have used it as the base for a stew, a sauce for tarts, rice cakes and frittata, a topping for Indonesian pancakes, part of a filling for a dolma dish as well as an accompaniment to another dolma. This, I think I'm trying to say, is a very versatile relish. The ingredients here constitute the full-on version, with the leanings of both east and west left in, while in practice I would often vary the recipe depending on the main use for the relish at the time. For example, if I am serving it with a late summer frittata of squash and feta, I will leave out the ginger and add some fresh herbs at the end, probably basil or oregano; if it is to be served with an Indian-oriented rice cake, I might take out the rosemary and add some whole cumin seeds. Either way, I will still take some home on a Sunday night and eat it with fresh pasta.

The recipe makes much more than you need to feed four people, but it keeps for days in the fridge, and how else can you discover its wonderful versatility unless you have a stash of it in the fridge?

FOR FOUR:

500g aubergine
olive oil
2 sprigs rosemary
2 onions, chopped finely
4 cloves garlic, chopped finely
2 teaspoons grated fresh ginger
2 teaspoons coriander seeds, ground
4 dried bird's eye chillies, ground
2 sprigs thyme
5 fresh tomatoes
120mls red wine
2 teaspoons tomato purée
salt, to season

120g fresh linguine per person
Parmesan, to serve

Chop the aubergine into small dice, put them in an oven dish and toss them in enough olive oil to coat them. Add the whole rosemary sprigs, and roast the aubergine in a moderate to hot oven, stirring occasionally, until the aubergine is browned and cooked through. Discard the rosemary stalks.

Heat two tablespoons of olive oil in a pan and cook the onion for five minutes, then add the garlic, spices and the leaves from the thyme sprigs. Cook for two minutes more. Chop the tomatoes into small dice and add them to the pan with the red wine and the tomato purée. Bring it to a boil and simmer for 20 minutes or more, until the sauce is reduced and thickened. Add the roasted aubergine and cook for a further ten minutes, stirring occasionally to ensure the sauce is thickening but not sticking. Season with salt.

Bring a large pot of water to a boil and cook the linguine for a few minutes until just tender. In a wide pan, gently heat two tablespoons of aubergine relish and one of olive oil per person. Drain the pasta, add it to the aubergine relish, and stir to coat the pasta. Serve with some finely grated Parmesan.

Aubergine wraps of pinenuts, spinach and Coolea cheese with a fresh tomato, thyme and caper sauce

I've called these things many a name in their day – today, they're wraps, but they've also been mere 'parcels', 'open ravioli' (a tad pretentious), 'foldovers' (literal, I'll use that again) and a few others; every name will cause someone to wrinkle up their nose and say 'but they're not…'. It's an occupational difficulty of having ditched the formal French food vocabulary, and can sometimes make a minefield of communicating what a dish on a restaurant menu actually is.

As delicious and perfectly matched as the flavours in these wraps are, the dish is really all about texture; and the texture depends on the cheese. When it works really well, the layers of shaved cheese melt – no, soften – into a luscious pillow that melts in the mouth. The roasted aubergine slices are wrapped around a mound of spinach, which is crammed with pinenuts and sweetened with the intensity of dried tomatoes. Now, if you grate the cheese and stir it through the spinach too, you will have all the flavours of the dish; but it won't be the same. You could spend the best part of a long wet evening thinking about the mysteries of that, and the melting properties of fine cheeses. In fact, this dish was created to try to grasp at that perfect moment in the melting of mature Coolea cheese. As I mentioned earlier it is a Gouda-style cheese made in Coolea in mid-Cork, a fun sandwich cheese at any stage of its life but a thing of sublime beauty at a year and a half old. All good Gouda melts beautifully, but there is a stage in the melting where the cheese has left its raw state behind, when it is warm and soft but hasn't yet become runny or stringy, and hasn't quite taken on the flavour of cooked cheese. There – catch it just there! Now do that with a cheese with the rich and complex flavour of mature Coolea… mmm… heaven. If you can't get Coolea, search out a good mature Gouda and keep going back for more – cheesemakers thrive on devoted fans.

I would usually serve these wraps with some grounding, earthy carbohydrates such as parsnip chips, or a simple potato, polenta or risotto dish.

The wraps can be made up and left to sit for an hour or two while you get on with the rest of the meal, and the final cooking will then only take ten minutes.

FOR FOUR:

4 medium aubergines
olive oil
400g spinach
60g pinenuts
2 tablespoons olive oil
4 sundried tomatoes
salt and pepper, to season
160g mature Coolea cheese or similar

6 tomatoes
2 cloves garlic
2 teaspoons small capers
2 sprigs thyme
3 tablespoons olive oil

Cut a slice from two sides of each aubergine, then cut the remaining flesh into three slices from each aubergine, four if they're very fat. You will need a few extra slices to allow for burning, accidents and sheer greed. Brush these slices lightly with olive oil and roast them in a hot oven until fully cooked and lightly coloured.

Bring a large pot of water to a boil, drop in the spinach and cook it for one minute, then remove it to a bowl of cold water to stop the cooking. When it is cooled, squeeze as much water as possible from the spinach and chop it coarsely. Toast the pinenuts lightly and chop them with a knife – you want them to be roughly chopped but not ground, and a food processor will make too much powder even if you're careful; another efficient method is to break them with a rolling pin. Chop the sundried tomatoes very finely and stir them into the spinach with the pinenuts and olive oil, and season it well with salt and black pepper.

Use a vegetable peeler to slice the cheese into thin shavings.

Place the aubergines on a work surface, best-looking sides down. Place some of the spinach-pinenut mix on one half of each slice, cover it with some shavings of cheese and fold over the other half of the aubergine to cover the filling. Place the aubergines on a parchment-lined oven tray and bake them in the oven, at 180°C/350°F, for ten minutes or so, until the cheese has just melted into soft pillows, but hasn't become runny. Serve the wraps immediately.

To make the sauce, first peel the tomatoes. Cut a small cross into the base of each tomato and drop them into boiling water for a few seconds, then plunge them into cold water. The skins should slip off easily. Cut the tomatoes in half, scoop out the seeds and cut out any green stem. Chop the remaining flesh into small dice and put them in a small pan. Chop the garlic finely and add it to the pan with the capers, the leaves from the thyme sprigs and the olive oil. Heat the sauce gently until boiling, then simmer for one minute. Serve immediately.

Aubergine, potato and fennel stew with red wine, thyme and chillies, and goats' cheese gougères

I first made this on one of those lovely autumn days that can cheer up a nation and make it forget an endlessly disappointing summer. We were coming home from a few days' kayaking, walking and drinking in West Cork with Bridget's parents and a few other globetrotting New Zealanders. I headed home before the others to get some dinner ready while they took in a few beaches on the way, as is the way of the kiwi. It had been on my mind to do something impressive for ma and pa, something I could serve with braised fennel, which I love to cook, but when I realised how many were coming home, and how hungry they were likely to be, the menu changed to something more substantial. In such circumstances, there's nothing to beat the old double-starch routine: in this case a stew containing potatoes served with lots of grilled crusty bread. Instead of making something elegant with aubergines and serving it with a sauce, potatoes and braised fennel, I cooked the vegetables and made a sauce to stew them in. Both the aubergines and the fennel are cooked in quite a bit of olive oil, which makes the stew very rich.

The stew is put together like a lot of stews I do, in that the vegetables are prepared separately and brought together in a sauce for a relatively short time. The idea is to have a full-bodied background of rich, deep flavours, while the vegetables in the stew retain their own distinct taste and texture. The aubergine and fennel also add to the flavour of the sauce, but I have deliberately chosen a firm potato that will hold its shape, in contrast to how potatoes often work to thicken the sauce in stews. The variety here is Nicola, a French potato I think, which I use a lot. It has a lovely yellow flesh with a rich, sweet flavour, clean thin skin, and is somewhere in the middle of the starch scale, making it suitable for just about everything, even a passable, though not Irish-mammy-standard, mash. If you make the stew well ahead of dinner, put the vegetables into the sauce but don't simmer it. Instead, simply reheat it gently when you need to.

Although I think of the sauce as primarily a wine- and herb-flavoured one, I throw in some chillies – just enough to add their mouth-warming quality to the rich, comforting nature of the stew. I also like the way chillies work with some herbs, especially thyme as here, but also basil, mint, fennel and coriander. Indeed one of my favourite stews from my early cooking days was a Caribbean-style dish flavoured with coconut, chillies and lots of fresh thyme. I must dig that one up again now I've remembered how good it was.

Use a fruity red wine for the sauce, a Merlot perhaps, or a Sangiovese or even an easy-drinking Portuguese from periquita grapes, as I used the first time I made it. I also drank the rest while the stew cooked, but that's not always necessary.

Although originally served with bread, the stew is a little more elegant with the choux pastry gougeres in this recipe. The gougères are best made to order, but they freeze well and can be reheated in a moderate oven. Any goats' cheese will do, but the drier and harder it is the better, to avoid making the pastry too wet.

FOR THE STEW:
3 fat bulbs fennel
150mls olive oil
*500mls vegetable stock
(see page 137)*
2 large aubergines
*500g potatoes, roosters,
Nicola or similar*
6 tomatoes
6 cloves garlic, sliced
2–4 fresh chillies, sliced
2 sprigs thyme
300mls red wine
salt, to season

Trim the greens off the top of the fennel bulbs, and slice a thin sliver off the root end, then slice the bulbs into quarters. Place them in a pot with 100mls of olive oil and 200mls stock, bring it to a boil and simmer for five minutes before transferring the contents of the pot to an oven dish (it would be even better if you start with a pot that can go in the oven). Cover the fennel loosely with parchment and place it in the oven at about 180°C/350°F. It should take about an hour for the fennel to become tender, but check occasionally that there is enough liquid, and you may need to turn some of the fennel pieces.

Slice the aubergines in quarters lengthways, then into large chunks. Toss these in olive oil in an oven dish and roast them in the oven for about 15 or 20 minutes, until soft and browned, turning them occasionally, but being careful not to break the pieces.

Wash the potatoes, but leave the skins on, and chop them into pieces about the same size as the aubergine. Steam the potato pieces until just tender.

Halve the tomatoes and slice them thickly. Heat some olive oil in a large pan and add the tomatoes, garlic and chillies. Cook them for a few minutes until the tomato softens a little, then add the whole thyme sprigs, the wine and the other 300mls of stock. Season with a little salt, bring to a boil and simmer for 20 minutes. Add the fennel in all its oily juice, the aubergines and potatoes, bring it back to a boil and simmer again over very low heat, covered, for 15 minutes. Check the seasoning before serving.

Serve generous portions of the stew surrounded by a few gougères (see below).

FOR THE GOUGÈRES:
170mls water
60g butter
2 eggs
80g goats' cheese

Put the flour in a food processor. Bring the water and butter to a rolling boil in a small pan and tip it quickly into the flour, with the motor running. After 30 seconds crack in one egg, wait 30 seconds again before adding the second egg, then add the cheese after a further 30 seconds. Once the cheese is incorporated into the dough, use a spatula to put the dough into a piping bag. Pipe small mounds of the dough on to parchment-lined oven trays, then put the trays in an oven at 190°C/375°F. After eight minutes, turn the oven down to 180°C/350°F, and turn any gougères that are cooking unevenly. The gougères should have puffed up to almost twice their size. Cook for another five minutes, or more, until they are firm and dry. Serve warm.

Roasted aubergine rolls with sheep's cheese and almond stuffing, and a Turkish pepper sauce

In the manner of the old truism about skinning cats, there's more than one way to stuff an aubergine. This variation on the theme uses two different-sized slices of roasted aubergine to hold a simple, classic filling of sheep's cheese, almonds and fresh coriander. I originally used the filling to stuff a halved aubergine, which was first roasted, then stuffed, and then the skin was carefully peeled off before the stuffed aubergine was roasted again. I did it for all those timid folks out there who leave aubergine skins on their plates, which drives me crazy; but the other cooks mocked its bald appearance and made rude remarks at it. Sometimes, the flesh would turn a dark grey between roastings, not an attractive colour in the food world, and in the end I had to admit it probably wasn't the most beautiful aubergine dish we'd ever done. If I crack the colour thing, I'll be back to it, though.

Anyway, this recipe is as much about the pepper sauce as the aubergine. There was a little mischievousness in naming it Turkish pepper sauce: when people asked what it was that made the sauce Turkish, I could say 'it's made from Turkish peppers'. And that is exactly what it is, or at least what it originally was – sauce made from Turkish peppers. The first time I put it on the Café Paradiso menu, I simply used olive oil and water to dilute the powerful pepper sauce that Sevinc brought back from a trip home.

Sevinc says her mother's sauce is a little heavy on texture because she doesn't peel the peppers, which makes her a lazy housewife where she comes from, but every culture has its own judgement system and, in mine, anyone who makes vats of pepper sauce is a hero. Her method I find hard to write down, because I find it hard to believe. Take some ripe peppers, Turkish ones that are hot and sweet from the sun, chop them, season with salt and place them in a large vessel. Cover the peppers with a few layers of muslin and put the vessel out in the sun for a few days – as long as it takes. Stir the peppers occasionally, and discard any from the top that may be going off instead of cooking… honest. When the peppers are sun-cooked, bring them indoors, stir in some olive oil and pack the sauce into jars. Try that in Ireland and you'll end up with peppers floating in barrels of rain. In attempting to duplicate the flavour using Spanish peppers and indoor cooking equipment, I've added chillies for heat and smoked paprika for that sun-roasted effect. Serve the aubergines with a green vegetable – green beans perhaps – and some potatoes or a grain dish such as couscous or basmati rice.

FOR FOUR:

2 sweet red peppers

2 teaspoons sweet paprika

4 dried bird's eye chillies, sliced

2 cloves garlic, sliced

200mls olive oil

100mls water

2 large aubergines

olive oil

1 red onion

2 cloves garlic

1 tablespoon cumin seeds

30g breadcrumbs

60g almonds

200g sheep's cheese, such as Knockalara, or use feta

1 small bunch fresh coriander

Blacken the skins of the red peppers under a hot grill or over a flame, then put the peppers into a paper bag until cool enough to handle. Peel off the skins and scrape out the seeds. Put the flesh into a pan with the paprika, chillies, garlic, olive oil and water. Boil for two minutes, then blend with a hand blender until the sauce is emulsified. Leave the sauce to cool and dilute to a pouring thickness if it seems too thick. Check the chilli heat and add a little more if you think fit.

Cut a slice from opposite sides of each aubergine, then slice the remaining flesh into four slices from each aubergine. Brush the slices lightly on both sides with olive oil and roast them in the oven until soft and lightly coloured.

Finely chop the red onion and garlic, and fry them in a little olive oil with the cumin seeds, until soft. Add the breadcrumbs and cook for one minute more. Toast the almonds briefly in the oven and chop them quite finely. Crumble the sheep's cheese and chop the coriander, then gently mix these with the almonds and the cooked onion.

Place the four smallest aubergine slices on a work surface. Place some filling down the centre of each, piled about 2cm high but leaving an edge of almost 1cm all around. Place one of the remaining slices of

aubergine over each, best-looking side up, and press it down all round the edges to enclose the filling. Place the filled aubergine on an oven tray lined with baking parchment, and bake them in a moderate oven for 10 to 15 minutes.

Serve one aubergine roll per person, with some of the pepper sauce at room temperature poured over.

Salad of grilled figs with pecans, rocket and watercress, mascarpone and a vanilla-citrus dressing

There's always a little battle of tug-o'-war in the Paradiso kitchen when the figs arrive. My supply is from a French organic grower, through an importer, so the figs are expensive, the season is brief and the supply a little erratic. Not through anyone's fault, it's just that ripe figs are fragile and don't travel well. Because of these factors, especially the cost, I only use figs when they are irresistibly good. There is sometimes an early supply of green figs in summer, which has never impressed me much, so I ignore those. Then in early autumn come the dark purple figs with deep-red flesh, just barely firm enough to be handled, perfectly ripe and sweet. Now that we're happy to pay for the figs, the issue is whether we can get enough to put a sweet and a savoury dish on the menu or if we'll have to compromise on one; if it's to be one, who gets the figs? Oh, I can pull rank on the pastry cook, but I've never liked the side-effects of pulling rank – it always comes back to haunt you. Sometimes I'm allowed to get my way and, if I do, I serve the figs in some variation of this salad – grilled, with some peppery leaves, a sweet-spiced dressing and mascarpone. Little dollops of mascarpone, dipped in olive oil, are lovely with salad greens, and with figs.

We get our watercress from Hollyhill Farm in West Cork, where it is not so much grown as managed and monitored in a pond fed by a running stream. Most years, when the heat of the summer is fading, there is a second crop that can survive until the first frost. If you have access to such a crop, lucky you; otherwise use rocket leaves or any mildly bitter or peppery leaves such as endive or mizuna.

FOR FOUR:

1 vanilla bean
rind of 1 orange
juice of half an orange
juice of 1 lemon
1 teaspoon fresh thyme
200mls olive oil
2 tablespoons pecans
150g rocket
150g watercress
10–12 ripe purple figs
80g mascarpone

Slice the vanilla bean in half lengthways and scrape the pulpy seeds into a jug or jar. Add to this the orange, lemon, thyme and olive oil, and use a hand blender to emulsify the dressing. Alternatively, put a tight lid on the jar and shake it vigorously until the dressing emulsifies. If it separates again later, simply shake it again just before you use it. Lightly toast the pecans in a moderate oven, leave them to cool and toss them with the salad leaves.

Heat a heavy frying pan or griddle pan to fairly hot and brush it very lightly with olive oil. Slice the figs in half and cook them briefly, cut sides down, until lightly singed – 20 or 30 seconds should be enough.

Toss the leaves in a little of the dressing and share them out on to individual plates. Arrange the figs on the salads. Use a teaspoon dipped in olive oil to drop a few blobs of mascarpone on each salad plate, then drizzle a little more dressing over everything and serve.

Cardamom and orange-roasted figs with amaretto semi-freddo

When you cook figs, think of where they come from and the images in your head will suggest the flavours that figs are happiest with. Warm exotic spices, citrus, almonds, honey… the recipes write themselves and, if only they would cook themselves, we'd never leave the table.

Semi-freddo is nothing more daunting than almost-frozen ice cream, though in restaurants it is more likely to be frozen ice cream that has been allowed to soften a little in the fridge before serving. For me, fresh – that is, before storage freezing – is the best way to eat ice cream. Freezers don't preserve food in perfect condition for even a short time; something is always lost in the process. Ever since working in an ice cream shop in New Zealand that made its own ice cream every day, I've had a thing about fresh ice cream. The best ice cream I've ever eaten was scooped with my fingers from the 20-litre churn we used; next day the ice cream was a frozen product, its irresistible magic gone.

FOR FOUR:

300mls milk
3 egg yolks
60g caster sugar
200mls cream
2 tablespoons amaretto liqueur

8–12 figs
6 cardamom pods
2 tablespoons unsalted butter
rind and juice of 1 orange
1 tablespoon honey or sugar

Heat the milk to just short of boiling for one minute. Whisk the egg yolks and sugar together until thick and pale. Still whisking, on low speed, pour in the milk through a sieve. Return this egg and milk custard to the pan and simmer, stirring all the time, until it is thick enough to coat the back of a spoon. Leave the custard to cool before adding the cream and the amaretto. Churn in an ice cream machine until almost set.

Serve what you need from the machine, then churn the rest until fully frozen and store in the freezer

Heat an oven to 180°C/350°F. Make a deep cross cut in the figs, to halfway down. Split the cardamom pods and crush the seeds, discarding the pods. Put the butter in an oven dish with the orange, the cardamom seeds and two tablespoons of water. Put the dish in the oven until the butter has melted, then stir everything together. Stand the figs in the dish and use a spoon to baste them with the liquid. Put the dish back in the oven for 15 minutes, until the figs are hot and the juice bubbling. Carefully remove the figs and put them on serving plates. Stir the honey or sugar into the juice and spoon it over and around the figs.

Place a small dollop of semi-freddo in the opening of each fig.

Pumpkins

I fell in love with pumpkins on my first trip to New Zealand. I fell in love with lots of things then, but pumpkin has been a stayer. There was always a pumpkin in the cupboard, or more likely half of a huge one, wrapped in newspaper. We ate pumpkin almost every day, but rarely did anything fancy with it. No matter what fabulous dishes were served, roast pumpkin would be a side dish; more than that, it was the staple, the starch, and in many ways the real centre of the meal. The quality of the pumpkin would be discussed and fretted over. This is very similar to how the Irish eat potatoes, so I knew the rituals.

Even now, despite the endless variety of pumpkin dishes we cook in the restaurant, at home we usually prepare pumpkin the classic way by chopping it into chunks, tossing them in butter, or a mix of butter and olive oil, and roasting them in the oven. This basic method is very flexible and can be adapted to complement the rest of the meal. Pumpkin roasted in butter and olive oil is so comforting, so melt-in-the-mouth, that it is a perfect carrier of herbs or spices. Rosemary is excellent, whole sprigs tossed in at the start of cooking; sage is always good with pumpkin, but added later in the cooking; the same goes for thyme, which is even better paired with some lemon rind. Mind you, I tend to add spice to roast pumpkin more than herbs – I have a thing about spiking comfort food with a kick – and I generally prefer to

use just one or two spices at a time. Chillies, chopped or ground, can be added to the roasting at an early stage; whole cumin seeds or chopped coriander seeds are very good with chillies, while cumin seeds alone is one of my favourites – but then I love almost anything with cumin seeds; ginger is wonderful with pumpkin, added late in the cooking, and, again, some lime or lemon rind is good with the sweetness of ginger. Always add a generous pinch of salt – pumpkins, like all starchy foods, need salt. I couldn't possibly exaggerate how important pumpkins and squashes are to my cooking in Café Paradiso. It would surely strain my imagination beyond capacity to produce lunch and dinner menus through the long autumn and winter without pumpkins. More than that, it would depress me to have to live without them.

When I returned to Ireland, there wasn't a pumpkin to be seen, except for the monstrous Hallowe'en varieties that have too little flavour and too much water content to be of any interest as food. Life took a major upward swing when we found Hollyhill Farm, a small organic vegetable farm, or it found us, more correctly. The farm is currently owned by a New Zealand/Irish couple who know their pumpkins and who even produce New Zealand's favourite variety, the Whanga Crown. When Café Paradiso opened, I was still either roasting pumpkins or making soup of them. With my own kitchen and a steady supply, I came to see pumpkins as hugely inspirational raw material. Because of the way I work – whereby dishes are always focused on one vegetable; and how that vegetable is initially prepared, cut and cooked can form the idea for the dish – pumpkins open up a very wide range of options and creating dishes from them seems so full of possibilities. With pumpkins, there are so many ways to start. The colour alone is reason enough to include pumpkin as an element on a plate, as are the possibilities of texture and structure. Large, roughly chopped pieces with their skin on make fine dramatic roast pumpkin; peeled and chopped into small dice, the pumpkin can be roasted or steamed and made into frittata, pies, gratins, pancake or dolma fillings, as well as risotto and pasta; grated or chopped as thin as matchsticks is a good shape for spring-roll fillings or fried fritters; sliced in thin wedges makes pumpkin one of the best vegetables to cook as tempura, while a thicker slice coated in crumbs or batter makes a more substantial fried snack. Some squashes, the firm but less floury varieties like butternut, can be sliced and stir-fried. Steamed pumpkin can be mashed, or puréed in a food processor, which will be wetter. Puréed is best for soups, sauces and sweet dishes, while gently mashed gives a dry, fluffy finish that makes wonderful gratins, gnocchi, ravioli, kofta and, well, mash.

I hope my use of the words 'pumpkin' and 'squash' isn't too confusing. I think of pumpkins as having dense and floury orange flesh, autumn vegetables that store well into the winter; and squashes as being summer vegetables, lighter in texture and less intensely flavoured, grown to be eaten freshly picked. I'm not sure my use is always technically correct, but I know what I mean, my staff know what I mean and the floor staff in Paradiso are very patient at translating to the public. In essence, if it behaves like a pumpkin it is a pumpkin – except the butternut, which is dense and orange-fleshed but is always called a squash! I think my definitions are consistent with usage in New Zealand, where I learned the language of pumpkins. For a more technical view of the matter, have a look at the *Oxford Companion to Food*, by Alan Davidson. The gist of his pumpkin section seems to be that only big orange-coloured vegetables like the Hallowe'en pumpkins are actually 'pumpkins'; but then he allows that 'pumpkin' is a kind of pet name anyway, and furthermore, all winter squashes can be and are called 'pumpkins'. Follow that? So, at least we're agreed that everyone is confused on the matter.

There must be thousands of varieties of pumpkin out there, and I can't claim to have used more than ten. Whanga Crowns are a class act among pumpkins and would be most connoisseurs' favourite. Crowns are usually large, 4–10kg, with a hard but thin, smooth, grey skin and vivid orange flesh that is sweet, rich and floury but not mouth-dryingly so. Their crowning glory, as it were, is that they are almost solid,

with a relatively small seed cavity, making them wonderful store food. There is little worse than a pumpkin that is all thick skin and stringy seeds. Two other large varieties that have stored very well for us are the Australian Queensland blue, which is actually grey-green in skin colour and has very dense, dry flesh; and Sweet Mama, American I think, dark green and with good orange flesh. Both, however, have an annoying tendency for the skin colour to bleed an inch or so into the flesh, causing a lot of waste when colour is an important part of the dish.

The most conveniently sized pumpkins are the smaller, more user-friendly, varieties such as the orange-skinned Japanese varieties, like hokaido, hobacha and uchiki kuri, as well as the butternut squash. These come in sizes of 1–2kg, which makes them more suitable for supermarkets and domestic pantries.

One final thing: peeling pumpkins isn't always necessary, as the skin softens when roasted and is often deliciously edible in the way that potato skins are. However, if a recipe calls for peeling, do it very carefully, as it often requires force and can be dangerous. The best way to peel a pumpkin is to chop it into halves, quarters or even smaller pieces and to use a sharp knife to slice the skin off, always pushing the knife away from you and down.

Roasted butternut squash with chickpeas and cumin

Roasted butternut squash holds its shape better than any other squash or pumpkin, which is why it is so popular in restaurant kitchens. That and its wonderfully rich orange colour. Although not as dry in texture as some of the other orange-fleshed pumpkins, butternuts still have an intense, sweet flavour. It isn't my favourite, but butternut certainly has its place and its uses. This dish, a simple variation on roast pumpkin, is one of them. The roasted squash is doused, just before it finishes cooking, in an oily combination of chickpeas and spices. The quantities don't really matter, how spicy you make it is up to you, but the proportions do – there should be just a scattering of chickpeas through the squash. I serve squash this way as a side dish to mildly spiced cabbage dolmas or spring rolls.

FOR FOUR:

1 small butternut squash, approx 1kg

olive oil

4 scallions

1 fresh red chilli

4 tablespoons cooked chickpeas

1 tablespoon cumin seeds

150mls vegetable stock or water

large pinch salt

1 small bunch fresh coriander

Peel the squash, slice it in half and scoop out the seeds. Chop the flesh into two-bite pieces, toss them in olive oil in an oven dish, and roast them in a moderate to hot oven until tender and beginning to caramelise at the edges.

Slice the scallions into long diagonal pieces; slice the chilli into thin rounds. Put these in a pan with the chickpeas and the cumin seeds. Add two tablespoons of olive oil and 150mls of stock or water, and a large pinch of salt. Bring this to a boil, simmer for one minute, then pour the contents of the pan over the roasted squash. Return the dish to the oven for five minutes. Stir in the fresh coriander before serving.

Spinach ravioli of pumpkin, basil and Gabriel cheese with lemon and black peppercorn butter

For these ravioli, and for most dishes that involve mashed pumpkin, it's important to start with the right pumpkin: one with dry flesh of an intense orange colour and sweet, rich flavour. To get the best of that flavour, I cook the pumpkin without water, by roasting it, and mash it gently by hand to get a dry, fluffy texture. All going according to plan, the ravioli filling will be no more than pumpkin flavoured with basil, snuggled up to some Gabriel cheese, needing no eggs, breadcrumbs, flour or anything else to bind or hold it together. The cheese is draped over the pumpkin mash in thin shavings, so that, when the ravioli are cooked, the cheese will melt into a lovely soft, distinct layer over the pumpkin. As well as the textural effect this gives, I like the way the flavours remain distinct yet together, rather than blended into one. The sharp, peppery flavour of mature Gabriel works very well with pumpkin, as will any full-flavoured and mature Gouda- or Gruyère-type cheese.

The sauce is a very simple one of clarified butter flavoured with lemon and a few cracked peppercorns. Don't grind the peppercorns or the whole dish will be too uniformly spicy – rather, split them (or buy cracked peppercorns), to provide the occasional thrill.

FOR FOUR STARTERS:

500g pumpkin flesh
olive oil
1 small bunch fresh basil
salt and pepper, to season
100g Gabriel cheese, or
similar

2 sheets fresh spinach
pasta, approx 16cm x
60cm

12 black peppercorns
80g clarified butter rind
and juice of 1 lemon

Peel the pumpkin carefully, scoop out the seeds and chop 500g of the flesh into large pieces. Toss these in a little olive oil and roast them in a hot oven until soft and lightly coloured. Mash the pumpkin with a fork or potato masher to get a smooth but dry mash. Don't overbeat the pumpkin or the mash will become too wet to stay inside the ravioli.

Chop the basil and stir it into the pumpkin mash. Season with salt and pepper.
Use a vegetable peeler to shave thin slivers from the Gabriel cheese.

Lay the pasta on a work surface and cut out two sets of circles, one slightly larger than the other, 12 of each size. From the size of pasta sheet given, one circle of 8cm and one of 7cm would be perfect, but do whatever best suits the pasta size and your cutting equipment. Take a smallish amount of the filling, small but as much as you think the parcel will hold – perhaps a teaspoonful – roll it into a ball and place it in the centre of one of the smaller circles of pasta, and press it gently to flatten it a little. Place three or four of the cheese shavings over the pumpkin. Brush the visible part of the pasta circle with water and place one of the larger pieces of pasta on top. Now press the edges together firmly while, at the same time, taking care not to leave any air pockets inside the parcel.

Repeat this with the rest of the parcels – you will need three each for a starter, more for a main course.

Make the lemon-black peppercorn butter before you cook the ravioli. Crack the peppercorns by laying them on a chopping board and pressing them with a rolling pin or the flat side of a knife, so that the peppercorns crack into large pieces but don't crumble to powder. Put the cracked pepper in a pan with the butter, lemon rind and juice. Heat it gently just before you serve the ravioli.

To cook the pasta, bring a large pot of water to a boil and drop in the ravioli. If you think the parcels might be overcrowded, do two batches. As with all pasta, the only way to decide that it's cooked is to test it, so nick a tiny bit off one of the ravioli and taste it. Remove the ravioli with a slotted spoon and put them in a bowl with a little olive oil to prevent them sticking to each other. If you do two batches, tip the first one back into the pot just as the second batch is cooked and remove the lot in half a minute.

Serve the ravioli on warm plates and spoon a generous amount of the butter over each portion.

Pumpkin gnocchi with spinach in a roasted garlic cream

We make gnocchi from either potatoes or pumpkins and so, having never tried to make the semolina flour-based version, I tend to think of gnocchi as a vegetable dish more than a pasta. Granted, it is necessary to add some flour to hold the show together… and the pieces of dough are boiled in water and served in a sauce… very pasta-like behaviour, yet I persist in my possibly skewed thinking. This attitude lost me most of my credibility one lunchtime in a fabulous and famous Italian restaurant in London when, while negotiating the short menu to concoct a vegetarian meal, I ordered a salad, then a starter of potato gnocchi in walnut and sage sauce, followed by a pasta dish in olive oil. I was pleased with myself and excited about the meal ahead, but the waiter was aghast and felt he had to save me from the inevitable disaster of lunching on serial pasta dishes. I argued that I was having a potato dish and a pasta dish made mainly from wheat; he pointed out, helpfully and sincerely for my benefit, that they were both in the section headed 'pasta' and were therefore pastas. Like all good waiters, having done his best, he gave me what I wanted without conceding his position. But I would bet my good leg that he had to argue my case for me in the kitchen and that there were a few eyebrows thrown skywards. Bloody English, he probably thought; I should have explained that I was Irish and that we never eat a meal without potatoes and that if they weren't available boiled in their skins we'd make do with gnocchi.

Still without conceding the argument, another thing that gnocchi has in common with pasta is that it can be served in a cream sauce or an olive oil-based one. I do a few different pumpkin gnocchi during the season and I serve some in robust, almost stew-like sauces with tomatoes, greens and olive oil; and sometimes I use rich but simpler cream sauces like this garlic cream.

If it is important to start with a pumpkin of dry, orange flesh when making ravioli, it is even more so for gnocchi. The gnocchi are made from a dough of mashed pumpkin and flour, flavoured with grated Parmesan and anything else you fancy; and the intention should be to use as much flour as is needed to hold the dough together, but to use as little as possible! Which is why you should take the measurements in this recipe as a guide only. It helps, too, to mash the pumpkin gently and to incorporate the flour with a light touch – think pastry making rather than bread kneading. Rough handling can make the dough wetter and in need of more flour, and can cause a tough finished texture.

Gnocchi need to be cooked soon after being made but uncooked ones keep well in a freezer if tossed in flour – rice flour is better for this than wheat flour, as it is much less inclined to be incorporated into the gnocchi.

Serve this gnocchi dish as a starter, and follow it with whatever you feel like, bearing in mind that gnocchi is quite a filling dish… like pasta.

FOR FOUR:

500g pumpkin flesh
salt and pepper, to season
100g flour
80g Parmesan

8 cloves garlic
olive oil, to coat
100mls light stock (see page 137)
100mls white wine
300mls cream
1 tablespoon chopped chives

100g spinach

Chop the pumpkin flesh into chunks and roast them in a moderate oven until tender, then mash them carefully with a potato masher, to get a lump-free mash but without over-pounding the pumpkin, which will cause it to become too wet. Season the pumpkin well with salt and pepper, then leave it to cool completely before carefully folding in half the flour. Mix in the flour by hand, then test whether the dough is firm enough to roll. If not, add some more flour until it is, bearing in mind that the less flour you use the better your gnocchi will taste. When you feel that the dough is right, fold in 60g of the Parmesan. If you have had to add more than 100g of flour, you may want to also add extra Parmesan and more seasoning. Roll a small piece of dough into a ball and drop it into boiling water to check the texture. If the ball holds its shape and floats to the surface after a few minutes, it is cooked and your dough is ready to use. Tear off a piece of dough and use your hands to roll it into a long tubular shape, about the thickness of your finger, then cut it into pieces 2–3cm long. Keep the gnocchi tossed in rice flour to avoid them sticking together.

To make the sauce, slice the ends off the garlic cloves, coat them lightly in olive oil and roast them gently in a low to medium oven, about 150°C/300°F, until the garlic is completely soft. Squeeze the garlic from its skin and put it in a jug with the stock and white wine. Use a hand blender to purée these and pass the purée through a sieve into a pan. Bring this to a boil and simmer until the volume is reduced by half. Add the cream and simmer again for a few minutes until the sauce thickens to a nice pouring consistency – try some on the back of a wooden spoon to get an idea. Season with salt and pepper. While the gnocchi are boiling, reheat the sauce and add the chopped chives to it.

Bring a large pot of water to a boil and drop the spinach in for a few seconds, then remove it to a bowl of cold water. Squeeze the water from the cooked spinach and chop it coarsely.

Drop the gnocchi into the boiling water, but don't overcrowd them – do a second batch if necessary. The gnocchi are done when they float to the top. Remove the cooked gnocchi with a slotted spoon. Place a generous portion of gnocchi on each of four plates, and pour some of the garlic cream over each. Place a few pieces of spinach on each plate and scatter the remaining Parmesan over. Finish the gnocchi by cooking them under a hot grill until the Parmesan melts, then serve immediately.

Butternut squash soup with lime and a coconut-peanut relish

Using butternuts instead of a dry pumpkin such as a crown or hokaido gives a finish that is more velvety than starchy, and can make a soup that is more elegant than substantial. Using a high proportion of onion in a potentially starchy soup like pumpkin or potato can also help to reduce the wallpaper-paste effect.

I use the coconut-peanut relish to provide contrast with the soup; whereas the soup is smooth, mellow and lightly spiced, the relish has bite, both in its texture and in its spicing, which should be hot if you have used hot chillies. If your chillies aren't hot enough, add a few dried hot chillies as well – it's important that there is a contrast between a mild soup and a hot relish, as there should be between a fiery hot soup and a cooling relish or cream. Lime juice is squeezed over the soup at the table for the same reason, as a sharp but pleasant contrast to the sweetness of the squash. If you like the relish, you will find that it is delicious with a lot of lightly spiced food, especially Indian and South Asian snacky things like fritters, pancakes, kofta and so on. Make the relish early on the day you need it, or a day before. It isn't a great keeper, however, so try to use it up in a couple of days.

FOR FOUR:

50g desiccated coconut
100g peanuts
2 hot red chillies, fresh
2 cloves garlic
juice of 1 lime
1 tablespoon sugar
large pinch salt

3 onions, chopped
1 medium butternut squash, about 1.2kg
1 tablespoon cumin seeds
1 tablespoon coriander seeds
1 dried bird's eye chilli
6 cloves garlic
1 tablespoon fresh ginger, grated
1.5 litres vegetable stock (see page 137)
200mls coconut milk
2 limes
large pinch salt

Soak the desiccated coconut in 200mls of hot water for 20 minutes. Roast the peanuts lightly in a low to medium oven, until lightly coloured, then chop them finely, almost but not quite ground.

Chop the chillies and garlic finely, and fry them in a little oil for two minutes. Add the peanuts for one minute, then add the coconut in its water, the lime juice and sugar, and a large pinch of salt. Bring this to a boil and simmer for two minutes. Put the relish in a bowl and leave it to cool. It should be slightly moist

Heat a little oil in a large pot and put in the onions to start cooking. Peel the squash, slice it in half and scoop out the seeds. Chop the flesh into chunks and add these to the pot once the onion has softened, and cook both together for five minutes. Toast the cumin, coriander and chilli in a small pan for a minute, then grind them finely and add them to the soup pot, along with the whole garlic cloves and the grated ginger.

Cook for two minutes before adding the stock. Bring this to a boil and simmer, covered, for 30 minutes or so, until the squash is soft and beginning to break up. Add all but two tablespoons of the coconut milk, the rind and juice of one lime and a large pinch of salt. Simmer for one minute more, then blend the soup to a smooth purée.

Ladle the soup into bowls and put a teaspoon of the relish on each. Swirl some of the remaining coconut milk into the soup and, finally, squeeze some fresh lime juice over.

Honey-roasted butternut with avocado-lime salsa, and green curry of cauliflower and beans

In general, squashes and pumpkins are large vegetables of haphazardly almost-round form. There are exceptions and, if I find any smaller squashes with interesting shapes, I try to maintain some element of that shape in the cooking. The simplest examples are those that are small enough to be stuffed whole or in halves, or the spaceship-like pattypans. The shape of butternut squash, with its elegant oval upper half ending in a round, bulbous base on which it sits, seems a partly dramatic and partly comic appearance, sometimes both and sometimes just one.

Slicing the squash into long wedges, as in this dish, preserves the dramatic element, even if it loses the comic. I'm not sure I'm ready for comic food anyway. Here, the butternut is cooked very simply, roasted with a glaze of honeyed butter, which gives a lovely caramelised sheen to it. The honey does boost the natural sweetness of the butternut, and that's why we serve it with an avocado salsa heavily laced with lime.

The green curry has a degree of sweetness too, though coconut milk is nothing like as sweet as the concentrated creams you can get in tins or pressed blocks. Mostly, the curry is a combination of hot chillies and ginger with lots of fresh herbs, coriander and basil, and it is the herbs that give it that lovely fresh and vibrant quality. The curry recipe is a combination of a few I found in the Café Paradiso notebooks when trying to pin down one definitive version to be used in the restaurant. It seems like we use a new variation every year, under the influence of travelling cooks and glossy magazines, so I'm making no claims of authenticity or correctness. It's a damn fine curry, though.

Serve some simple boiled basmati rice with this dish, to mop up the curry and prop up the roasted butternuts.

FOR FOUR:

1 large butternut squash, about 2kg, or 2 smaller ones

2 tablespoons clarified butter

1 tablespoon clear honey

1 leek, white part only

2 teaspoons cumin seeds, ground

1 teaspoon fennel seeds, ground

60g fresh ginger

5 bird's eye chillies

1 bunch fresh coriander

1 bunch Thai basil, or any basil

400mls coconut milk

1 small cauliflower

200g runner beans

4 scallions

salt

1 clove garlic

1 lime

1 avocado

1 tablespoon olive oil

Peel the squash with a vegetable peeler, slice it into quarters lengthways, and scoop out the seeds. Slice each quarter in half again lengthways to get eight long wedges. Melt together the butter and honey, brush the squash wedges with it and place them in an oven dish. Roast the squash in a moderate oven, at about 180°C/350°F, until tender and lightly browned, turning them once or twice to cook evenly.

Chop the white of the leek and put it in a food processor with the cumin and fennel seeds, the ginger and chillies. Blend to a smooth paste and remove it to a container. Put the herbs in the processor and chop them finely, then add the coconut milk and blend to get a nice green milk.

Break the cauliflower into florets, then slice these into halves or quarters. Slice the beans

and scallions into long diagonal pieces. Heat some oil in a wok or large frying pan and fry the cauliflower for a minute before adding the green beans. Cook these together for two minutes before adding the scallions and the paste. Continue to fry for two or three minutes, then pour in the herbed milk and a pinch of salt. Bring the milk to a boil for one minute, then serve immediately.

Crush the garlic clove and put it in a small bowl with the finely grated rind and juice of the lime and a pinch of salt. Dice the avocado flesh and stir it in with one tablespoon of olive oil.

Serve the curry with some basmati rice, and lean two wedges of butternut squash on each portion. Spoon some avocado-lime salsa into the well of the squash.

Roast pumpkin, onion and feta tart in walnut filo pastry with cucumber and yoghurt sauce

There was always going to come a point in this book where I would have to eat my words on the subject of filo pastry, and this is as good a recipe as any to take a stand on. While acknowledging that it is one of the most useful materials in the professional catering world, it is its very convenience that also makes it responsible for some lazy, bland cooking. At least the words that need to be temporarily swallowed are not mine but those of an unidentified Turkish cook whom I quoted earlier as praying that 'creative' chefs be kept away from filo pastry. Okay, I agree most days and for most dishes, but the thing is that this is a wonderful pie in the honourable tradition of pies, and I have tried to make it with other pastries but none works as well as filo. I think the only other one that would work is that old English 'hot-crust pastry' that we used in Cranks in the early 1980s to make a wonderfully earthy pie, almost 10cm high and filled with root vegetables and winter herbs. Even so, the semi-open top of this pie can only be achieved with filo. The effect justifies the means, perhaps? I scatter some coarsely ground walnuts between the sheets of pastry, partly for their flavour and partly to help the pastry to stay separate and crisp. After that the filling is a simple matter of pumpkin and feta cheese laced with what I think are my top-drawer spices, the ones I would take to a desert island and which, by an extraordinary coincidence, go very well with pumpkin. So I guess I'd take a pumpkin plant as well.

FOR ONE TART
(ENOUGH FOR SIX):

800g pumpkin flesh
600g onions
olive oil
6 cloves garlic, coarsely chopped
2 teaspoons cumin seeds
2 teaspoons coriander seeds, ground
1 fresh chilli
240g feta cheese

80g butter
1 packet filo pastry

80g walnuts, coarsely ground
4 eggs
150mls cream

Chop the pumpkin flesh into dice of about 2cm, toss these in a little olive oil and roast them in a moderate oven until soft and lightly coloured.

Slice the onions in half, then into short, thickish slices. Heat a little olive oil in a pan and cook the onions and garlic together for ten minutes, stirring often, until the onion is very soft. Add the cumin, coriander and chilli, and cook for another five minutes, then stir this into the roasted pumpkin. Crumble the feta into pieces roughly the same size as the pumpkin and fold it in gently.

Melt the butter, and butter a 26cm spring-form tin. Lay a sheet of filo pastry on a worktop, with a long side facing you as the bottom edge. Cut it into three pieces from top to bottom. Brush the pastry with butter, scatter some ground walnuts over half of each piece and fold them in half to get three long strips. Place one in the tart tin, starting at the centre, coming up the side and over-hanging the top. Place the second strip in the tin in the same way, slightly overlapping the first. Continue with the third piece, then repeat with more pastry until the tin is fully lined. Pile in the filling and pack it gently.

Beat the eggs with the cream and pour this custard over the filling. Fold the overhanging pastry over the top of the tart, folding the strips back on themselves once or twice and leaving the centre of the tart uncovered. Brush any unbuttered pastry with butter and place the tart on an oven tray in a moderate oven, 180°C/350°F, for 40 minutes or so, until the filling is set and the pastry lightly coloured. If possible, cook this in an oven without a fan to avoid burning the pastry. Leave the tart to sit in the tin for ten minutes before removing the side of the tin and slicing the tart carefully.

1 medium cucumber

2 scallions

2 cloves garlic

2 tablespoons chopped
fresh coriander

1 tablespoon chopped
fresh mint

400mls thick plain
yoghurt

salt and cayenne pepper,
to season

Slice the cucumber in half lengthways and
scoop out the seeds. Roughly chop the
cucumber and the scallions, and put them in
a food processor with the garlic and herbs.
Add three tablespoons of the yoghurt and
blend until you get an almost-smooth purée.
Use a spatula to move this to a bowl or jug
and stir in the rest of the yoghurt. Season
with a little salt and a small pinch of cayenne
pepper.

Gratin of roast pumpkin, leeks, sweetcorn and hazelnuts with a Gabriel cheese cream

There are dishes that are wonderful to eat but that could never be sold in restaurants, usually for aesthetic or legal reasons. At the opposite end of the spectrum, there are dishes that could exist only in restaurants and have no function in the real world. The ultimate embodiment of this is the very famous restaurant in Spain that contorts a little food and a lot of air into mindbendingly brilliant creations held together with gelatine, egg white, ice, sugar, water, magic spells and what-not; and where the clientele are mostly other chefs and bored gourmets in need of impressing while the public stubbornly go on eating for pleasure and good company.

Further in on the scale, the scene is a bit blurry and dishes overlap and slip from one side to the other, and get adapted to make them work in the other setting. Some domestic dishes are never as good in a restaurant, usually because they have to be prepared in a different way; some restaurant dishes don't turn out quite so well at home.

Occasionally, the way a restaurant adapts a simple dish from home can actually improve it. I think this gratin is one. At heart it's a basic domestic crumble, where the vegetables are bound with a sauce in a large oven dish, covered with a crust and baked in the oven. Which is where the rings come in. You will need four steel rings of about 8cm diameter and 3cm high.

The rings are indeed a restaurant affectation, their prime function being to hold individual portions in a uniform shape that looks good on a plate. But cooking individual portions for a shorter time, and cooking the sauce separately, also allow the elements and the flavours of the dish to be held together yet remain distinct in flavour. All going well, the dish is no longer a simple one-taste comfort food, it is more sophisticated both in its appearance and flavour. The crust, the vegetables and the rich Gabriel cheese sauce get along all the better for being distinct.

Serve a vegetable dish with the gratin – one that looks good on the plate. Some green or broad beans cooked with tomato and garlic are good, maybe some fried cabbage or other greens, or, as we often serve in Paradiso, little spoonfuls of braised lentils or cannellini beans as on page 114.

80g hazelnuts

40g fine breadcrumbs

2 tablespoons melted butter

1 tablespoon chopped chives

salt and pepper, to season

120g Gabriel cheese, grated

400g leeks

4 cloves garlic, coarsely chopped

2 tablespoons butter

half glass white wine

1 teaspoon Dijon mustard

2 sprigs thyme

120mls cream

600g pumpkin flesh

olive oil

2 ears of sweetcorn

50mls vegetable stock (see page 137)

50mls white wine

200mls cream

Roast the hazelnuts in a low to medium oven for 30 minutes or so, until they are toasted through but only lightly coloured. Rub the nuts in a damp towel to remove the skins, then break them gently under the side of a knife or a rolling pin. You should get halves and quarters of hazelnuts in the mix as well as smaller pieces. Stir the nuts into the bread-crumbs with the melted butter and chives, and season well with salt and pepper. Finally, add 40g of the grated Gabriel cheese.

Wash the leeks carefully, and cut them in half lengthways, then across into slices about 1cm thick. Melt the butter in a large pan, and cook the leeks and garlic in it, over high heat, until the leeks are just tender but still bright green. Add the wine, mustard and thyme, and cook for three minutes more, then add the cream and boil it for two minutes. Pour the leeks into a wide bowl to cool.

Peel the pumpkin, unless the skin is very thin, and chop the flesh into dice of about 1.5cm. Toss the pumpkin pieces in a little olive oil and roast them in a moderately hot oven until the pumpkin is tender.

At the same time, boil the sweetcorn until tender, then use a sharp knife to scrape the kernels from the core. Break up the very big pieces but don't fret about breaking it all down to individual kernels.
Gently stir both the pumpkin and the sweet-corn into the leeks.

Place your four steel rings on an oven tray lined with baking parchment. Fill each with the leek and pumpkin stuff, gently pressing it in. Spoon some of the hazelnut crumble over each one and press it down firmly. Bake the gratins in an oven at 190°C/375°F for 15 to 20 minutes. The top should be lightly browned and the filling heated through.

At the same time, bring the stock and white wine to a boil in a small pan, and boil for two minutes before adding the cream. Bring it back to a boil and simmer for two minutes before stirring in the Gabriel cheese and a little salt and pepper. Allow the sauce to boil for just a few seconds before serving.

Use a serving slice to lift the gratins on to individual plates, then lift off the rings. The gratins should hold up fine without the support. Pour the Gabriel cream around each gratin and serve. If you are serving a vegetable, put three small spoonsful around each portion.

Baked pumpkin, cashew and yoghurt curry

Pumpkins take on spices beautifully, especially in slow-cooked dishes like this simple curry. Eat the curry with rice or Indian bread for a simple meal but, if you can, make at least one other dish. A tomato-based dish with lots of chillies will give the contrast you need.

The pumpkin is boiled briefly before baking, partly to speed the cooking but mostly because the warm and slightly softened pumpkin pieces will absorb the spices better.

FOR FOUR:

100g whole cashews

1kg pumpkin flesh

1 medium leek

1 tablespoon olive oil or butter

3–4 fresh green chillies

1 tablespoon grated fresh ginger

1 tablespoon cumin seeds, ground

1 handful fresh coriander, chopped

500mls plain yoghurt

200mls cream

large pinch salt

Heat an oven to 150°C/300°F, and roast the cashews for 15 minutes or so until lightly coloured but cooked through.

Peel the pumpkin and chop the flesh into large pieces. Drop these into boiling water for three minutes until partly cooked.

Slice the leek in half lengthways, wash it well, and chop it into thickish slices. Heat a tablespoon of oil or butter in a large, wide pan and cook the leeks for three minutes. Slice the chillies thinly and add them to the leeks with the ginger and cumin, and cook for one minute more. Add the part-cooked pumpkin, the cashews, fresh coriander, yoghurt, cream and a large pinch of salt, and stir gently to combine everything. Transfer everything to an oven dish and place in the oven at 150°C/300°F to cook slowly for 30 to 40 minutes, until the pumpkin is tender and the yoghurt sauce has become drier.

Chickpea, leek and rosemary soup with a hot pepper salsa

Leeks make such a wonderful base for soup that everybody's got a leek soup of one kind or another. Most of them are a variation on the classic and almost unbeatable leek and potato soup, which, up until recently, you could find in every bar, bistro and fine restaurant the length and breadth of Ireland, given a run for popularity only by the worryingly non-committal 'vegetable soup'. Although occasionally you might have come across a mean-spirited one that was all cheap potato and cheaper water with a mere hint of leek, the soups were (and still are) generally well made from raw ingredients by people who understood leeks and potatoes. Leek and potato soup on a blackboard menu outside a pub meant comfort, warmth and nourishment against the rain and cold. Okay, sometimes it never came off the menu, even in the summer, and you might have suspiciously wondered where the leeks came from then. Now, 'leek and potato' is gradually being replaced by soups thought to give a more modern image, notoriously 'tomato and basil'; and I can assure you that the mild surprise of finding leek and potato soup in summer is nothing to the horror of finding 'tomato and basil' after a long trudge in the misty Irish countryside in winter. If it's not made with tinned tomatoes and dried basil, it's sure to be green Dutch tomatoes and, well, nothing else. Grown, bearded and muddied men crying into their watery tureens is an awful sight.

As well as their old friend, the spud, leeks also make great soup with carrots, parsnips or turnips. There is a lovely soup I made for years in another restaurant, which went by the slightly pretentious name of 'Crème Andalucia'; it was a variation of a Spanish leek, tomato and potato soup, which had been given a French twist with the addition of tarragon and cream. It was fantastic, and a huge hit, but I left the recipe behind and have never tried to make it since.

Leeks have a lot of natural sweetness, which can be too much if combined with another sweet ingredient like carrots or parsnips, in which case it is a good idea to add a little lemon juice at the end of cooking; or swirl some soured cream or yoghurt into the bowls of soup for balance.

The almost automatic tendency to add potato to leek soups can give the impression that leeks make thick, comforting soup. This is not necessarily true – indeed, a simple leek soup with white wine, herbs and a little cream or olive oil can be a very elegant and light first course. This recipe for chickpea, leek and rosemary soup can go either way, though I prefer to rein in its comfort-food tendencies by keeping the proportion of leeks to potato and chickpeas high. It started life as a very simple chickpea and rosemary soup, which was surprisingly delicious, even if poor-sighted customers of Café Paradiso occasionally thought they were being promised a herbed broth of fowl bones.

The soup is only partly blended, which is achieved by removing some of the vegetables before blending and putting them back into the blended soup. This is one of many tricks I use to give texture to soups without spending hours chopping kilos of vegetables into tiny pieces. As much as I, in my caterer's hat, like to sell easily made blended soups, I know that, as a consumer, I get bored after a few identical spoonfuls, and only a ferocious hunger could make me go on. If I don't leave some

texture in a soup, I like to serve it with a salsa, some sautéed vegetables or croûtons. This recipe has two such textural effects: the soup is only half-blended and the hot pepper salsa adds not only texture but a dramatic flavour to be taken in small or large doses with each spoonful as you wish. By such diversions do we get to the end of our soup bowl with appetite intact.

....

FOR FOUR:

2 tablespoons olive oil
2 onions, chopped
600g leeks
5 cloves garlic, chopped
100mls white wine
150g peeled potatoes, chopped into small dice
150g chickpeas, cooked
1200mls stock (see page 137)
3–4 sprigs rosemary
salt and pepper, to season

2 peeled red peppers
2 cloves garlic
4 bird's eye chillies
2 tablespoons olive oil
rind and juice of half a lime

Heat two tablespoons of olive oil in a large pot and cook the onions until soft. Slice the leeks in half lengthways, wash them well and chop them across into thin slices. Add the garlic to the pot with the leeks, and stew everything together for five minutes. Add the wine and cook for five minutes more. Add the potatoes to the pot with the chickpeas, the stock and the whole rosemary sprigs. Bring this to a boil, and simmer for 30 minutes.

With a slotted spoon, take out about one-third of the vegetables, throw away the rosemary sprigs, then use a hand blender or food processor to blend the rest of the soup to a fine purée. Put back in the vegetables you took out, season well with salt and pepper, and gently reheat the finished soup.

While the soup is cooking, or before, chop the peeled peppers into fine dice, chop the garlic and chilli finely and put them in a pan with the olive oil and the lime. Heat for one minute, then leave the salsa to cool to room temperature before using it.

Ladle the soup into bowls and swirl a generous amount of salsa into each one.

Leek and blue cheese tartlet with roasted cherry tomatoes

Up to mid-autumn, the focus tends to be on freshly picked or dug vegetables, and all energy and attention is concentrated on getting them in their prime and using them at their best. As these fresh foods fade away, the emphasis switches to vegetables that store well or grow slowly, leaving a wide window of time in which to harvest them. Then, leeks gradually become the most versatile and most used vegetable. From late autumn through the freezing winter and into spring, the leeks sit in the ground, ready and waiting to be picked. Eventually, at the first warming of the ground, any leeks still in the ground bolt, their cores becoming woody and unusable. Chances are that, by then, you've just about had enough of them. That's an element of seasonal eating I enjoy – the putting away until next time of a vegetable you love but have gorged on for long enough.

During this time, leeks find a role in so many dishes, often combined with other vegetables, sometimes used almost anonymously as though they were onions. We cook them with pasta and noodles, in omelettes and fritters. They're used in soups, stews, stir-fries – in fact, just about any dish using two or more vegetables is likely to include a leek or two.

Occasionally, it's all about the leeks. The natural sweetness of leeks gives them a great affinity with cheeses. I particularly like them with lightly smoked Gubbeen, the rich and peppery Gabriel, goats' cheeses of all styles and ages, and the softly melting Goudas and Gruyères. But it's the simple sweetness and acidity balance, I think, that makes a nice creamy mature blue cheese as good a partner for leeks as you'll get. That's all there is to this tart – a perfect combination of leeks and mature Cashel blue in a crisp buttery pastry. I serve it sitting on sweet, roasted cherry tomatoes balanced with a touch of balsamic vinegar, and a few peppery leaves of watercress or rocket, whichever is available. I have sometimes served a pesto with it but it's a sauce too far, to be honest. Keep it simple, the flavours are perfect.

FOR SIX TARTLETS:

150g plain flour
large pinch salt
75g cold butter
40mls cold water

400g leeks
2 cloves garlic, chopped
1 tablespoon butter
half teaspoon Dijon mustard
1 tablespoon chopped chives
salt and black pepper, to season
100g blue cheese

400g cherry tomatoes
drizzle of olive oil
2 teaspoons balsamic vinegar

Sift the flour and salt together. Cut in the butter. A food processor does this very efficiently, but remove the pastry to a bowl before stirring in the water with a few quick strokes. Shape it into a ball with your hands, flatten it gently and chill for at least half an hour. Roll the pastry and cut out circles to fit six small tartlet cases of about 7cm diameter. Prick the pastry cases all over with a fork and chill them again for 30 minutes, then bake them for eight to ten minutes at 180°C/350°F until crisp. Check after five minutes in case the pastry has puffed up in places; if it has, press it gently back in place while it is still soft.

Slice the leeks in half lengthways, and wash them well, then slice them thinly. Melt the butter in a wide pan and cook the leek and garlic over high heat for about five minutes, until the leek softens but retains its colour. Add the mustard and the chives and cook for one minute more. Season with coarsely ground black pepper and a small pinch of salt.

Fill each pastry case three-quarters full with the leeks, without packing too hard. Crumble some blue cheese on top and bake the tartlets at 180°C/350°F for eight to ten minutes, until the leeks have warmed through and the cheese has melted.

Halve the cherry tomatoes, put them in a small oven dish and sprinkle over a little olive oil and some salt and pepper. Roast the tomatoes in the oven for eight to ten minutes, until softened a little. Add the balsamic vinegar for the last minute of cooking.

Spoon a pile of roasted tomatoes in their juice on each plate and place a tartlet on top.

Corn pancakes of leek, parsnip and Gabriel cheese with a cherry tomato-fennel salsa

We've been using these corn pancakes for a few years to wrap various fillings. They're made from a variation on a classic crêpe batter, with a few spices thrown in and most of the wheat flour replaced by maize meal. You may know maize meal, which is very finely ground maize or corn, as corn meal; you may even know it as corn flour, but calling it that will only lead to confusion with the very fine white starch powder used for thickening, also derived from corn, and known as cornflour. Besides its colour and flavour, the reason I use maize meal is the way it helps the pancakes to become crisp in the oven.

Leeks and parsnips make good soup, so it makes sense that they would get on well in other dishes, and they work very well here with the strong, peppery Gabriel cheese. The way the leeks are cooked for the filling is a method we use for a lot of leek dishes. The chopped leek is cooked over very high heat so that it goes soft in a short time but without leaking too much liquid or losing its lovely pale green colour, which it will do if a large volume of leek is stewed slowly. The leek is then quickly flavoured with thyme, mustard and wine, and then bound together with some cream. The technique was perfected by John Healy, who used to put a large pot on a very hot flame and go do something else for ten minutes before starting on the leeks. One evening, one of the other cooks put one, just one, teaspoon of ground chilli into the pot, causing a minor outbreak of coughing and eye-rubbing in the kitchen as the chilli vaporised, seeming to poison the air. Gradually, the dining floor staff began to splutter, and then the nearest diners; it was with a combination of horror and amusement that we listened to the seemingly contagious coughing move slowly through the dining room, right to the tables by the windows on to the street. It was 15 minutes before things returned to normal though – because there was no smell, nobody outside the kitchen fully realised that there was a single cause for the outbreak.

The cherry tomato-fennel salsa that I serve with the pancakes is another variation on what would be my favourite taste on most days – the heat of chillies with naturally sweet vegetables in warm olive oil. It's great with cheese dishes.

Serve two pancakes as a main course with the salsa, some potatoes or rice, and a simple green vegetable or salad.

120g fine maize meal
80g plain flour
pinch ground turmeric
pinch cayenne pepper
large pinch salt
3 eggs
450mls milk
olive oil

500g leeks
300g parsnips
1 tablespoon butter
3 cloves garlic, coarsely chopped
50mls white wine
1 teaspoon Dijon mustard
2 sprigs thyme
80mls cream
100g Gabriel cheese

1 small fennel bulb
1 fresh red chilli
2 cloves garlic, finely chopped
200g cherry tomatoes, halved
4 tablespoons olive oil
pinch salt

Sift the maize meal, flour, turmeric, cayenne and a large pinch of salt together. Whisk the eggs and milk together, then whisk them into the flour to get a smooth pouring batter. Heat a crêpe pan, brush it with olive oil and swirl in just enough batter to coat the pan. Cook the pancake for a minute or two and flip it over to cook the other side for a minute. The batter will make 12, but you need only eight (two each), so you have room for a few failed, stuck or burned pancakes.

Wash the leeks carefully, and cut them in half lengthways, then across into slices about 2cm thick. Peel the parsnips and grate them on the widest and thickest grater. Melt the butter in a large pan, and cook the leeks and garlic in it, over high heat, until the leeks are just tender but still bright green. Stir in the grated parsnip, cook for one minute, then add the wine, mustard and thyme, and cook on high for three minutes more, then add the cream and boil it for two minutes. Pour the leeks into a wide bowl to cool. If the heat is high enough and you have worked quickly, the leeks should be quite dry.

Grate the Gabriel cheese and stir it into the cooled leeks.

Place a pancake on a work surface, best-looking side down, and cut a slice off the bottom, about 2.5cm up, and a similar slice from the top. Place two tablespoons of the leek filling along the bottom edge and roll up the pancake tightly, pressing the filling as you go so that it fills the full length of the tube you are forming from the pancake. Repeat with the rest of the pancakes, then place the filled pancakes on an oven tray, lined with baking parchment. Brush them with olive oil and bake them in the oven at 190°C/375°F for ten minutes, until the pancakes are crisp.

Save any green fronds in good condition from the top of the fennel bulb, discard any stringy or discoloured leaves of the bulb and cut out the thick core. Chop the rest of the fennel into very thin, short slivers. Halve the chilli lengthways, then slice it thinly. Put the fennel, chilli, garlic and tomatoes in a small pan with the four tablespoons of olive oil and a pinch of salt. Bring it to a boil and simmer for one minute. Chop the fronds of fennel herb, and stir them into the salsa just before you serve it.

Serve two pancakes per portion, with some warm salsa spooned over each.

Risotto of leeks, butternut squash and sage with pumpkinseed oil and braised lentils

Butternut squash risotto is becoming quite a common dish on restaurant menus, but what interests me about this recipe is the way it uses the white and green parts of the leeks in different ways. The whites are finely chopped and used in the role usually played by onions at the start of the cooking of the risotto; the green tops of the leeks are stewed in olive oil and added to the risotto at the end of cooking, as a featured vegetable. The presence of sage and braised lentils rounds off the warm, autumnal feel of the dish, both being flavours that I often use with pumpkins and squashes.

When writing this recipe, I had just rediscovered a toasted pumpkinseed oil I had lost track of over a year previously. Having struggled on manfully, occasionally using an insipid French oil instead, I was moaning one day about the lost oil to a class I was giving. A woman in the class went off and came back with a few tablespoons of the oil in a little jar and, more importantly, the address of the makers. Turns out it was an Austrian oil, which I could never have remembered, and it was exactly as it had been in my hazy memory – an intense toasty flavour and the most amazing shade of green, which seems almost black except when thinly spread on a white plate. I wrote to the makers explaining my plight and they posted six large bottles, without payment upfront. Such trust, but so much oil! So, now I'm in the pumpkinseed oil business, if anyone's interested.

FOR FOUR:

400g peeled butternut squash

olive oil

1 large leek

1400mls vegetable stock (see page 137)

60g puy lentils

4 cloves garlic, chopped

1 sprig thyme

rind of 1 lemon

salt and black pepper, to season

60g butter

60mls olive oil

320g risotto rice, such as arborio or carnaroli

120mls dry white wine

6 leaves sage, chopped

60g Parmesan, grated

2 tablespoons toasted pumpkinseed oil

Chop the squash into 2cm dice, toss them in a little olive oil and roast them in a moderate oven until tender and lightly coloured.

Slice the leeks in half lengthways, wash them carefully and chop off the white ends. Slice the green tops of the leek about 1cm thick, and the whites much finer.

Bring the stock to a boil in a pot and keep it at a very low simmer.

Heat a tablespoon of olive oil in a pan and cook the lentils and two cloves of garlic together for two minutes. Add the thyme, lemon rind and stock, bring it to a boil and cook at a lively simmer until the lentils are just tender. There should be a little juice left, formed by the mingling of the olive oil and 200mls of the stock; if not, or if the stock boils off before the lentils are quite done, simply add a few spoons of stock at the end or at any stage of the cooking. Season the lentils with salt and black pepper.

Melt one tablespoon of the butter with one spoon of the olive oil, and cook the white of the leek for a minute. Add the rice and two cloves of garlic, and stir well to coat the grains with oil. Cook the rice gently for ten minutes, stirring often, then pour in the wine, bring it to a boil quickly, and simmer until the wine is absorbed. Now add a ladle or cup of the stock, and continue to simmer, stirring often until it is all but absorbed. Add another cup of stock, and carry on absorbing, stirring and adding stock until the rice is almost cooked. Take care that the stock going into the rice pot is at a boil and not, therefore, interrupting the cooking of the rice.

While the risotto is cooking, stew the leek greens for about ten minutes in a tablespoon of olive oil until just tender but still green.

Test individual grains of rice – they should be cooked through but firm, while the stock has become a little creamy and is almost completely absorbed. When the risotto reaches this stage, stir in the leek greens, roasted squash, chopped sage leaves, the remaining butter and olive oil, and the grated Parmesan. Season well with salt and pepper.

Serve the risotto with a little pumpkinseed oil drizzled over, some lentils in their juice scattered around each portion, and some Parmesan on the side, either finely grated or in a chunk to be shaved.

Roasted leeks with a lemon, ginger and pinenut marinade

Although leeks roast very well – in that they become soft, succulent and sweet – I've never been completely confident about the process because I've never found a way to do it that doesn't leave at least the outer leaves tough to slice through. There's something about the texture of a roasted leek that makes it tricky for a table knife. I've even tried out recipes from other people's books and they turn out the same. In my most recent attempts, I came up with this absolutely delicious version, which involves slicing the leeks in half lengthways into pieces about 10cm long. We ate the leeks with grilled haloumi, which always needs some lemon and olive oil, and roasted pumpkin. The leeks in their marinade did away with the need for a sauce for the haloumi, and set me thinking that the combination could be turned into an elegant starter. Then it went to the back of my mind and I haven't done it yet. Maybe someone else will, perhaps at a fabulous dinner party that I'll get invited to…
I put ginger in the marinade simply because I love ginger with leeks, but if you're worried that ginger will clash with the rest of your harmoniously balanced meal, change the marinade. Think of the marinade as essentially a lemon and olive oil combination, and then any herb or spice that goes well with leeks can be added to it – basil, thyme, garlic, chillies, fennel and rosemary are all good.

Roasting leeks this way also works very well with the baby leeks that appear occasionally in the summer, though the outer leaves will still be a little stubborn to table knives.

FOR FOUR:

4 medium leeks
drizzle of olive oil
salt
splash of water or stock
1 tablespoon pinenuts
1 lemon
1 tablespoon fresh ginger, grated
2 tablespoons olive oil

Cut the green tops from the leeks and save them for another dish. Slice the white parts in half lengthways and check carefully for dirt – wash the leeks if necessary, being careful not to break them up. Arrange the leek pieces in an oven dish with olive oil and a little salt, and roast them in a moderate oven for 15 to 20 minutes. Sprinkle a little stock or water over occasionally, to help the leeks cook without burning.

Lightly toast the pinenuts in the oven, then place them in a small pan with the rind of the lemon, the juice from half of it, the ginger and two tablespoons of olive oil. When the leeks are tender, heat the marinade and pour it over them. If you are transferring the leeks to a serving dish, do that before you pour the marinade over.

Winter

cauliflower

winter greens

pears

roots

potatoes

clementines

pineapple

store

blood oranges

Cauliflower and beetroot tempura with ginger-soya dip

There are vegetables that are good as tempura and vegetables that are not. Of those that are, some are actually improved by the cooking method, as though it reveals something in the character of the vegetable that wasn't obvious before. This is the best that cooking can achieve, and it is why I love tempura. So much of the time cooks who are lucky enough to have good produce strive to preserve the vegetables' qualities and to present them intact at the table. Sometimes, by the magic of cooking, hidden qualities are teased out. Some of the best vegetables to cook as tempura are pumpkin, broccoli, carrot, aubergine, oyster mushrooms and asparagus, but this pair – cauliflower and beetroot – is my favourite. They certainly look good together, but beetroot would look good anywhere, and its earthy sweetness is a nice contrast to the more elusive flavour of cauliflower.

I have carried out experiments on my children, cauliflower-haters to a man, on the matter of tempura and vegetables. Presented with a platter of vegetable tempura, they will avoid the aubergines and mushrooms because they don't like the vegetables and tempura hasn't changed them; they will eat the carrots and broccoli because they like carrots and broccoli; they will eat the beetroot grudgingly, admitting its nicer than they expected, but they will eat the cauliflower because it makes the best tempura. And this isn't a case of children eating anything deep-fried because it all tastes the same; tempura batter is too thin to hide the nature of the food it coats.

Naturally, these experiments were carried out under gentle, caring conditions and no children were hurt or injured in the process.

It is essential to cut slices of even thickness from the cauliflower, even when this seems to involve cutting cross-sections from the rounded florets, which may seem wasteful. However, frying rounded slices of cauliflower, or any vegetable, in tempura will result in uneven cooking and undercooked centres. This is especially true of both cauliflower and broccoli, the loose florets of which can hold half-cooked batter, which is particularly nasty to eat.

The beetroot must be sliced thinner than the cauliflower so that it will be cooked through in the short time it takes the batter to crisp.

FOR FOUR:

150mls soy sauce
2 tablespoons saki or sherry
1 tablespoon grated ginger
100mls water

half a medium cauliflower
1 largish beetroot

225g plain flour
2 egg yolks
375mls iced water

Stir together in a jug the soy sauce, saki, ginger and water.

Break the cauliflower into large pieces, keeping the florets intact. Use a sharp knife to cut flat slices 5–6mm thick.

Wash the beetroot and, without peeling it, slice it into thin rounds or half-rounds, no more than 2mm thick.

Heat a deep fryer to 190°c/375°f.
Put the flour in a bowl and add the egg yolks, then whisk in the cold water to make a thin batter.

Drop some of the cauliflower and beetroot pieces into the batter. Lift one slice out, gently shaking the batter from it so it has just a thin coating, then carefully slide it into the hot oil. Put in as many slices as will comfortably fit in the fryer without overcrowding. Turn each slice once with tongs, and lift the slices out on to absorbent paper when they are crisp and very lightly coloured. If you need to do a second batch, leave the first on the paper until the second is just about cooked, then toss the first lot back into the fryer for the last few seconds of cooking. Serve the tempura immediately, either on individual plates or a communal platter, with separate bowls of the dip.

Cauliflower soup with green peppercorns and avocado oil

The flavour of raw cauliflower can sometimes be so robust, even spicy in a peppery way, that it is often shocking how that flavour can disappear in even the gentlest of cooking, especially in water. Cauliflower soup that involves quite long cooking in water can easily end up tasting of the support flavours and not at all of the cauliflower. With this in mind, I have tried to come up with a way to prepare cauliflower soup that tastes primarily of cauliflower, without being merely a purée of cauliflower. The cauliflower is braised briefly and blended with a potato-thickened stock. To add complexity without drowning the cauliflower, I add other flavours at the table. This version uses green peppercorns and avocado oil; herbs such as chives and fennel are good, as are nut oils, especially hazelnut.

FOR FOUR:

100g floury potato

1 small onion, chopped

2 cloves garlic, finely chopped

1 sprig thyme

800mls vegetable stock (see page 137)

1 large cauliflower, about 450g net weight

120mls white wine

salt, to season

2 teaspoons freeze-dried green peppercorns

1 tablespoon avocado oil

Peel the potato, chop it and put it in a pan with the onion, garlic cloves, thyme and stock. Bring the stock to a boil and simmer until the potato is soft and breaking up. Remove the thyme sprig and blend the rest to get a smooth, slightly thickened, liquid.

Chop the cauliflower into small pieces, put it in a pan with the wine, over low heat. Cover and braise the cauliflower for about five minutes until it is tender but not too soft. Add the potato stock, bring it to a boil and simmer for one minute. Blend the soup to a smooth purée and season with a little salt.

To serve, ladle the soup into bowls, crack some green peppercorns between your fingers and sprinkle them over the soup, then drizzle a little avocado oil on top.

Savoy cabbage dolmas of wild rice, leek and eggs in truffle oil

As best I can remember it, this came about from a brief and uncharacteristic obsession with hard-boiled eggs. Once you've gone there, it's a short step to eggs with truffle oil. The filling has a very loose texture, with nothing to bind it, so I cook the wild rice so that the grains soften and open up, which is more than if I was serving it as a grain in its own right.

Savoy cabbage isn't the most obvious leaf to use as a wrapping. With its crinkled texture, it can easily end up being a more substantial part of the dish than the filling. Even so, it's the one I like to use for this dish, for its flavour of course, but also because for a time in winter it's the best cabbage there is. So we persevere. First, we make sure the leaf is fully cooked in boiling water, not merely blanched; then the stem is trimmed to the thickness of the leaf; and finally the leaf is pressed completely flat. The leaf is now a suitable wrapping material, but there's more: as the leaf is rolled around the filling, any excess pieces are trimmed away. All of this seemingly laborious process is to get a parcel that is well sealed and contained, but that has only a thin layer of cabbage all around.

I don't usually serve a sauce with the dolmas. In Café Paradiso, we serve them cooked wet with the braised cannellini beans on page 114, wet so that they double as vegetable and sauce, and some parsnip chips. If you do want to serve a sauce, make a light cream sauce flavoured with fennel perhaps, or dill and a little mustard.

FOR FOUR:

60g wild rice
300g leeks
tablespoon butter
olive oil
2 cloves garlic, finely chopped
50mls white wine
1 sprig fresh thyme
1 sprig fresh fennel
50mls cream
4 hard-boiled eggs
12 savoy cabbage leaves
salt and pepper, to season
white truffle oil
a little vegetable stock (see page 137)

Cook the wild rice in boiling water until tender and the grains have opened a little, then drain it in a colander or sieve.

Chop the leek in half lengthways, wash it and chop it into thin slices. Melt a tablespoon of butter with a little olive oil in a wide pan and cook the leek and garlic over high heat for five minutes, then add the wine, the thyme leaves and the fennel, and cook for two minutes more. Pour in the cream and boil it for one minute, then add the wild rice, take the pan off the heat and transfer the cooked filling to a dish. When the filling has cooled, chop the hard-boiled eggs and stir them in. Season with salt and pepper.

Trim the stalks of the cabbage leaves with a sharp knife or vegetable peeler, to make them as thin as the leaves, and take a slice off the base to give a flat edge there. Bring a pot of water to a boil and drop in the cabbage leaves to cook for five minutes or so until fully tender, then drop the leaves into cold water to cool.

Lay a cabbage leaf on your work surface and flatten it with a rolling pin. Put a tablespoon of filling at the base, shaped to form a tube 8cm long. Sprinkle a few drops of truffle oil over the filling. Cut the corners off the leaf just outside this shape, about 6cm up into the leaf. Leaving a 4cm-long section in the centre at full length, repeat the cutting at the top of the leaf, to leave a cross-shaped leaf. Roll the leaf up around the filling from the base, fold over the side flaps of leaf and continue rolling, keeping the parcel as tight as possible. Cut off the end of the leaf when the parcel has been rolled one full turn after the middle.

Repeat this process with the rest of the leaves, then place the rolled parcels in an oven dish that has been brushed with olive oil. Brush the tops of the dolmas generously with more olive oil and sprinkle over some stock, enough to just cover the base of the dish. Loosely cover the dish with foil or baking parchment and place it in an oven at 190°C/375°F for 20 minutes, then remove the cover and cook for five minutes more.

Thai cabbage and onion soup with coconut, lime and coriander

This is about as basic as it gets, really: cabbage and onion soup. Every culture that has a cabbage or two has a cabbage soup. Whether a bread-thickened stew from the Mediterranean or a thin, spiced broth stretching a few leaves into a meal, cabbage soup is usually a way to feed whatever number of stomachs are present with the cheapest, possibly only, ingredients to hand. Food from the last ingredients in the kitchen or the only ones in the garden. You could say that, if you don't have some cabbage and onions left in the kitchen, then you're in bad shape. Well, you could, except that with the familiar becoming increasingly unfashionable you are now very likely to find a kitchen without cabbage while still well stocked with out-of-season asparagus and the ubiquitous broccoli. We are indeed out of sorts.

I called this a 'Thai' soup when I first put it on the Café Paradiso menu. Thai food was very fashionable, and still is. The word 'Thai' on a menu suggests certain flavours – coconut, citrus, chillies and fresh coriander being some – so the customers weren't disappointed; in fact, there was one who needed to be contacted when the soup was made. But the recipe is not derived from any authentic source, nor is it inspired by a dish eaten or seen. I mean that it is 'Thai' only in the widest sense; it is cooking in the general area of a style, not an attempt at authenticity. This brings together two potentially contradictory aspects of how I like to cook: working with local produce in its best season, and using flavours, methods and styles from all over the world. The second is a very common phenomenon these days; combining it with the first can bring out surprising characteristics in familiar ingredients, even give them a new lease of life. To me, this seems like much more fun than chasing down authentic ingredients to duplicate dishes out of context.

The onion and cabbage in the soup are cooked until just tender and the broth is heavily spiced and sweet, making the dish quite refreshing and invigorating. This freshness, by the way, makes it difficult to maintain on a restaurant menu because making a large batch (and restaurants love to make large vats of soup) will give you refreshing soup for an hour and stodgy soup for a day or two. Serve it fresh. Any leftovers will be fine tomorrow as a more comforting soup – try adding some beans, noodles or rice to make a substantial lunch of it.

FOR FOUR:

500g white onions

250g savoy cabbage

2–4 fresh green chillies

olive oil

4 cloves garlic, sliced

4cm piece ginger, finely chopped

1 tablespoon coriander seeds, ground

800mls vegetable stock (see page 137)

400mls coconut milk

1 bunch fresh coriander, chopped

large pinch salt

1 lime

Chop the onions in half, then into thin slices. Shred the cabbage leaves into similar slices. Slice the chillies into thin rounds.

Heat a little oil in a large pan, put in the onion and cabbage together and cook them over medium heat for three minutes before adding the chillies, garlic, ginger and coriander seeds. Continue cooking for about 15 minutes, stirring often, until the onion and cabbage are tender but not soft. Bring the stock to a boil in a separate pan, then add it to the vegetables and simmer for five minutes.

Add the coconut milk, half the fresh coriander, and a large pinch of salt, and bring the soup back to the boil.

Serve the soup in deep bowls with a scattering of extra coriander leaves and a generous sprinkling of lime juice.

Braised cabbage with fennel, tomato and chickpeas

Cabbage has historically been boiled, and well boiled at that, until the house took on and gave out the horrid smell. Digby Law, in his *Vegetable Book*, recommends to those who 'insist on boiling the hell out of cabbage' that adding a slice of bread soaks up the smell, almost accepting that it was a cultural battle that could never be won. How things change – now it would be easier to find someone to admit to having ever voted for Margaret Thatcher than to being a practising cabbage-boiler. We're all stir-frying and wilting these days. Me included. But, hey, here is a way to get lovely, soft buttery cabbage without stinking the house out. You can use any green cabbage. The recipe came about on one of those evenings when the only certainties for dinner were that it would involve cabbage and that there would probably be more people than currently present in the kitchen. To buy time, I started cooking the cabbage while trying to think of what to do next. I'm a very slow thinker in a domestic kitchen; in fact, Bridget usually has to give me clues like peeled potatoes and cracked eggs, or some spring roll pastry and a few carrots left on the bench. The cabbage was compulsory because it was my son Oscar's pride and joy – on a visit to the country that afternoon he had climbed a ditch and traipsed through a few rows of turnips to pick it out of a farmer's field with the permission of the farmer's next-door neighbour. Nice neighbours, eh? It wasn't the kind of cabbage I would usually give much attention to – a few huge tough green leaves wrapped around a tight head of smooth crisp leaves, which were a very pale green. Half an hour of cooking showed it to be sweet and delicious. We ate it with mashed potatoes, egg frittata and boiled turnips – yes, Oscar had also secured a huge turnip from the same field.

In dishes like this, which call for a small quantity of chickpeas, it is invariably too late to start cooking dried chickpeas, unless you are practised with a pressure cooker. I usually use tinned ones; it's a good idea to keep a few tins of organic chickpeas in the cupboard.

FOR FOUR:

300g cabbage

1 onion

1 small bulb fennel

2 tablespoons olive oil

2 tomatoes

4 tablespoons cooked chickpeas

100mls white wine

2 tablespoons butter

salt and pepper, to season

Quarter the cabbage and cut the core from the pieces you are using. Wrap any cabbage not being used in paper and keep it in the fridge or any cool place. Chop the cabbage into slices about 1cm thick. Chop the onion in half and then into slices half as thick as the cabbage. Halve the fennel bulb and slice it as thickly as the onion, discarding any stringy parts and the core.

Heat two tablespoons of olive oil in a large wide pan, and toss in the cabbage, onion and fennel. Cook over a medium heat, stirring often, for five minutes or more until the vegetables have softened a little. Chop the tomatoes into large dice and add them to the pan with the chickpeas and the wine. When everything is hot and bubbling again, turn the heat down to low, cover the pan and simmer for 20 minutes. Lift the lid occasionally to check that the vegetables aren't sticking, and add a splash of water or stock if necessary. Season well with salt and pepper before serving.

Wilted kale with garlic, puy lentils and thyme

Kale – common curly kale – is the king of winter greens, higher in my estimation even than savoy cabbage. Through the cold months I use kale in the way that I would ordinarily use spinach – in gratins, crêpes, pastries and so on. My favourite recipe of autumn and early winter is a gratin of gingered kale and pumpkin (from *The Café Paradiso Cookbook.*)

Mostly, however, I like to just wilt some kale in olive oil. There are a number of ways to dress up the basic model of wilted greens. Among my favourites are adding chickpeas, lemon and cumin, or a few tablespoons of cooked wild rice and red onions. In this recipe the kale uses the lentils as a flavouring, along with garlic and thyme, rather than a dish of lentils with some greens stirred in. Puy lentils are certainly substantial enough to be the main element of a dish but they are also intense enough in flavour to be a supporting element. This characteristic also makes them good scattered through pasta dishes, around risotto and in salsas.

FOR FOUR:

2 tablespoons puy lentils

2 tablespoons olive oil

1 onion, thinly sliced

4 cloves garlic, thinly sliced

2 large handfuls kale, roughly chopped

2 tomatoes, diced

2 small sprigs of thyme, leaves only

salt and pepper, to season

Boil the puy lentils in plenty of boiling water until just tender (about 12 minutes).

Heat a tablespoon of olive oil in a wide pan and cook the onion for one minute over medium heat. Add the garlic and kale, increase the heat and cook for two minutes until the kale has wilted and turned a dark glossy green. Add the tomatoes to the pan with the cooked lentils and the thyme. Continue cooking, stirring often and adding a splash of water occasionally, until the tomatoes are soft and the kale is tender. Add another tablespoon of olive oil at the end, along with salt and pepper to season.

Brussels sprouts with tomato, ginger and coriander

To many of us, Brussels sprouts are known only as neat little net sacks of vegetables on shop shelves at Christmas time. If only we could see them as the extraordinary vegetables they are: tight mini-cabbages sprouting along a tall brassica stalk with rampant greens at the top, like a cabbage gone crazy. I recently saw sprouts for sale at an American city market, the entire two-foot-long stalks laid out on trestle tables. They were so beautiful and striking that all passing shoppers and tourists were drawn to them, and you would think it was indeed a rare and exotic luxury that was for sale. I watched the sprouts sell like hot cakes and you can be sure they were lovingly cooked that evening, treated as the wonderful vegetables they are.

Brussels sprouts are available for a much longer season than the two weeks of glory usually granted them, but they are hopelessly linked with the annual feast. Any vegetarian who puts his head over the parapet – or indeed people of minority religions and those who go for solitary walks on 25 December – will be asked once or twice what he or she will be eating for Christmas dinner while the 'rest of us' are dining on tradition and nostalgia. Suggesting that Brussels sprouts are a pleasure can cause a mixture of rage and pity.

They divide people into lovers and haters as only fiercely individual vegetables can, and the lovers are further divided into those who like their sprouts cooked soft and those who like them crunchy. I take no sides here: I like them boiled soft or firm, puréed, fried, spiced and cold from the fridge at 3am. Whatever one's personal preference, it is undeniable that such a strongly flavoured vegetable can tolerate more robust cooking than plain boiling. Like most cabbages, sprouts are great with tomatoes, ginger and soy sauce. So this recipe is really nothing like as shocking as it might seem to annual sprout-boilers. Excellent as a side dish, it can also be made into a pilaf by adding some cooked rice, fresh coriander and maybe some toasted cashews.

FOR FOUR:

400g Brussels sprouts

4 tomatoes

1 tablespoon olive oil

1 red onion, thinly sliced

2 cloves garlic, thinly sliced

1 fresh chilli, thinly sliced

1 tablespoon coriander seeds, crushed

1 tablespoon fresh ginger, sliced

1 tablespoon soy sauce

Peel the outer leaves from the sprouts and slice the larger ones in half. Bring a pot of water to a boil and drop the sprouts in for just half a minute before removing them again.

Chop the tomatoes in half, then into thickish slices.

Heat a tablespoon of olive oil in a wide pan and add the sprouts and the red onion. Cook over a medium-high heat for two minutes, stirring, before adding the garlic, chilli, coriander and ginger. After another two minutes, add the tomatoes and soy sauce, and cook on a medium heat for five minutes more. Add a splash of water if the dish seems to be drying out – it should be moist when finished.

Vanilla-poached pears with cinnamon ice cream

I love the quote from Edward Bunyard in Alan Davidson's *Companion to Food* that, while it is the 'duty of an apple to be crisp and crunchable, a pear should have such a texture as leads to silent consumption'. Mind you, eating a very ripe and juicy pear can be a cacophony of slurping and sloshing, so either he is referring to a firm pear or he had very refined eating manners. More than apples, pears last well into the winter because they can be picked a little under-ripe and left to ripen in a cool place. Pears that are ripe but firm are perfect for poaching, in that they hold their shape and colour while absorbing the flavours of the poaching liquid. There are a few timeless flavours that complement pears, and vanilla and cinnamon are two of the best. Chocolate is almost universally accepted as another, though the case doesn't seem to be completely closed on that one yet. If you like chocolate with pears, a thin chocolate sauce would go very well with this dessert.

FOR FOUR:

FOR THE PEARS:
600g sugar
800mls water
2 vanilla pods
6 pears

Bring the sugar, water and vanilla pods to a boil in a small deep pan. Peel the pears and put them into the syrup. Simmer very gently for 20 or 30 minutes until the pears are just tender, then leave them to cool in the syrup. Serve at room temperature, with the cinnamon ice cream.

FOR THE ICE CREAM:
300mls milk
2 cinnamon sticks
3 egg yolks
140g light muscovado sugar
300mls cream

Put the milk and cinnamon sticks in a pan and heat slowly, almost to boiling. Whisk the egg yolks and sugar together until they are pale and thick. Pour the warm milk through a sieve into the sugar and egg, still whisking. Return this custard to the pan and heat gently until thickened a little. Strain this through a sieve into a bowl and leave it to cool. Add the cream and freeze in an ice cream machine.

Roasted roots and some uses for them

Although not a new idea, roasting roots has become very common and popular in the last decade or so. And for good reason, because the roasting transforms what are often perceived to be dull vegetables into sweet treats. It's not magic, rather that cooking by roasting draws out the natural sweetness of vegetables, and roots contain quite a bit of sugar, especially carrots and parsnips, but turnips too. Celeriac and salsify are relatively low in sugar and don't benefit much from roasting, though they can be worth including in a mix of roots for their distinctive flavours. Beetroots are, of course, very sweet and roast beautifully, but should always be cooked separately if you want to avoid a purple mess. While one type of root alone makes a nice roast, I think a pair is a little more interesting, and the best combination is the classic trio of carrots, parsnips and turnips. That last is the large yellow-fleshed turnip sometimes called a swede, as distinct from the little white summer turnips beloved of many restaurants. I don't understand the fuss about those at all, and have never found anything useful or tasty to do with them that couldn't be achieved by sucking on a golf ball. The swede turnip, or simply 'turnip' as it shall be called from here on, can have a wonderfully rich, sweet flavour. The colour of the flesh is a good indicator of quality, much as is the case with pumpkins: the yellower and denser the flesh, the better the flavour will be.

One evening in the Paradiso kitchen we tried, as an experiment, eating that other great root of the Irish countryside, the sugar beet. It was a quiet night and these little games get us through. We boiled a few slices and roasted some chunks, then gathered round sheepishly. It was one of the vilest things I've ever tasted, a nauseating combination of a kind of sickly sweetness, an earthiness that seemed to be from very deep down in a filthy field and a quality that I can only call oldness; it was like eating something from thousands of years ago. The taste, even from a small bite, wouldn't go away all evening and I suspect the memory never will.

You can roast roots in olive oil, clarified butter (see page 60) or a combination, as I like to do, simply because I like the taste of both butter and olive oil on roots. Garlic is excellent with roots, as are some herbs (the hardier ones such as rosemary, thyme or sage). Some red onion is good too, especially if you are going to use the roots in a pilaf or stew later (see below).

Although you can roast roots from raw, I think this can dry them out too much, so I like to boil them for a minute or two first. That way you get a crisp outside and a moist inside. To cook similar-sized pieces of different roots, it's a good idea to boil the longer-cooking roots for a few minutes more than the others and then roast them all together.

You will get the perfect balance of sweetness if the roots are roasted until the outsides begin to caramelise – beyond this point, the roots can easily burn and become bitter instead of sweet.

*1kg roots (carrots,
parsnips, turnips)*

1 head garlic

*4 sprigs rosemary, thyme
or sage*

Peel the roots, chopping medium-sized carrots and parsnips in half and bigger ones into large pieces. Chop the turnip into pieces of a similar size to the other roots. Bring a pot of water to a boil and drop in the turnip pieces to cook for two minutes before adding the carrots. Cook for one minute more, then add the parsnips and cook another minute. Drain the vegetables and toss them in an oven dish in just enough olive oil and/or clarified butter to coat them. Be careful not to use too much or the vegetables may fry instead of roasting. Peel the garlic cloves and toss them with the herbs through the vegetables. Roast the roots in a hot oven, about 200°C/400°F, for 30 minutes or so, until the roots are beginning to caramelise on the outside and are tender inside. Turn the roots a few times during the cooking.

Couscous pilaf

Fry some sliced red onion and chillies, cumin and fennel seeds in a generous amount of olive oil and add them to the roasted roots, with some soaked couscous, just less than the volume of roots. Serve the pilaf with fresh coriander scattered over and some accompaniments such as marinated feta, spiced chickpeas, toasted almonds, green beans with tomato and herbs, deep-fried felafel or other fritters.

Roasted roots gratin

Chop the roots into smallish dice rather than large pieces and use them instead of pumpkin in the recipe on page 189.

Roasted roots soup

Cook some onions until soft; add the roasted roots, a little chopped potato and some stock. Cook until the potato is soft, then purée the soup. Serve quite thick with some soured cream or yoghurt swirled on top.

Roasted roots mash

Mashed roots is a favourite food from my childhood, so it was inevitable that I would eventually try mashing some roasted roots. It's wonderful, but be careful not to roast the vegetables too much or their outsides will be too tough to mash. Boil about a quarter as much potato as you have roasted roots and mash it with plenty of butter. Blend the roots in a food processor, in short pulses, until the roots are very finely chopped but just short of puréed. Transfer them to a pot, stir in the potato and reheat to serve.

Coconut curry of roasted roots

Make a simple curry sauce by putting equal quantities of cream and coconut milk in a pan with some toasted and ground cumin, coriander and fennel seeds, turmeric, sliced green chillies and the rind of a lime. Heat gently and simmer for a few minutes until the sauce is slightly thickened, then add the roasted roots and some fresh coriander.

Risotto of parsnip, salsify and sage with beetroot crisps

When I first got a supply of salsify a few years ago, I thought I was in roots heaven, pleased with myself for having access to large quantities of an obscure root, a small team of cooks to prepare the things and time to play with ways to cook it. I enjoyed being generous with it. By all accounts, it's not easy to grow and it needs a good depth of soil to accommodate its length, which can be up to 40cm or more. In the stony soil of most of Ireland that would guarantee you some pretty weird, gnarly shapes, but in parts of Europe it thrives. It is hell to prepare too: it must be peeled without washing, preferably over an expanse of old newspapers, and quickly immersed in water with lemon juice added to prevent discolouring. No matter how fast you go, it makes a fierce mess and gives off a sticky sap that causes all the loose dirt from the outer skin to stick to your hands and the lovely creamy inner flesh that you're trying to keep from discolouring. Or so the boys tell me – I avoid the chore if I can. However, I still admire salsify's unique, subtle flavour and the vegetable's admirable persistence in surviving in these times of convenience when awkward species are dying off at an alarming rate. I have learned to buy small quantities of salsify and to use it sparingly, as in this risotto, where it is paired with parsnip, another root with a fine individual character.

Roast parsnip is delicious in risotto but salsify doesn't roast well, so rather than cook the roots in two different ways, we compromise and fry them together in butter until lightly browned.

Beetroot crisps are delicious and fun, both to make and to eat. Because the crisps shrink a bit in the cooking, you need a fine big beet to cut slices off, and you will probably need a mandolin slicer to cut uniformly thin slices. The ideal thickness is the second thinnest setting on the mandolin, which I'm afraid I can't translate into millimetres. The slices need to be kept separate from each other in the fryer, and if you do this quite busily you will get some lovely chaotically curved crisps. The crisps will keep for a few days in a tightly sealed container.

FOR FOUR:

FOR THE CRISPS:
1 large beetroot
salt and pepper, to season

Slice the beetroot into very thin slices, as large as possible, using a mandolin slicer if you've got one. Heat a deep fryer to 170°C/340°F and put in a batch of the beetroot slices. Stir frequently to encourage even cooking and prevent sticking, until the oil becomes calm and the beetroot appears cooked. Tip out the slices on to kitchen paper, season with salt and pepper and leave them in a warm part of the kitchen to become crisp.

FOR THE ROOTS:
200g salsify
juice of half a lemon
200g parsnip
1 medium leek
1 tablespoon butter
1 tablespoon olive oil
4 cloves garlic, chopped
6–8 sage leaves

Peel the salsify with a vegetable peeler and drop the pieces into cold water with lemon juice added to prevent discolouring. Peel the parsnips, chop out and discard the core. Chop the flesh of both roots into small pieces. Bring a pot of water to a boil and cook the parsnip until almost tender, then remove it and cook the salsify to the same stage.

While the risotto is cooking (see below), wash and chop the leek. Melt a tablespoon of butter and a tablespoon of olive oil in a pan and cook the salsify, parsnip, leek and garlic over moderate heat for ten minutes, stirring often. Tear the sage leaves, add them to the pan and cook for a few minutes more until the roots are tender and lightly coloured.

FOR THE RISOTTO:

1200mls vegetable stock (see page 137)

60g butter

60mls olive oil

320g risotto rice, such as arborio or carnaroli

120mls dry white wine

60g Parmesan, grated

Bring the stock to a boil in a pot and keep it at a very low simmer. Meanwhile, melt one tablespoon of the butter with one tablespoon of the olive oil, and toast the rice in it for eight to ten minutes, stirring often. Pour in the wine, bring it to a boil quickly, then simmer until the wine is absorbed. Now add a ladle or cup of the stock, about 150mls, and continue to simmer, stirring often until that is all but absorbed. Add another cup of stock, and carry on absorbing, stirring and adding stock until the rice is almost cooked. Take care that the stock going into the rice pot is at a boil and so not interrupting the cooking of the rice. Test individual grains – the rice

should be cooked through but firm, while the stock has become a little creamy and is almost completely absorbed.

When the risotto reaches this stage, stir in the cooked roots and leek, take the risotto off the heat and stir in the remaining butter and olive oil, and the grated Parmesan. Add a little stock to the pan that the roots were cooked in and bring it to a boil. Serve the risotto with these pan juices poured over each portion, some beetroot crisps on the side and some more Parmesan to sprinkle or shave on to the risotto.

Carrot and chestnut cannelloni with watercress cream

Like most people, we use carrots all year round. Carrots go into stocks and soups, in the Monday-night stir-fries when you can't decide whose turn it is to cook, in fritters for the children, and in pasta dishes when pasta is only an excuse to make them eat all the vegetables in the fridge. And carrots are the best all-round multi-purpose side dish: a bowl of cooked carrots, however dressed, will be welcome on any table, no matter what the main dish. Some people will swear that carrots are best eaten raw and no amount of cooking will improve on that. Others insist that only baby carrots are worth any special attention, and they certainly do make a lovely sweet contribution to salads and other dishes in the summer. But when I want carrots that really taste intensely of that sweet and rich flavour of carrot, I look for the really big ones with a deep orange colour. Carrots grown to maturity in comfortably yielding soil. Some vegetables seem very Catholic in their need for a bit of stress and hardship in their lives; they may like a touch of frost or thin, undernourished soil. Not carrots. Carrots are guilt-free hedonists and thrive only if you pamper and pleasure them.

This cannelloni recipe is not the classic way of making the famous pasta dish. Instead of baking the filled tubes in a sauce, the cannelloni are only heated through in the oven as they are already warm inside and out, and the sauce is added on the plate.

When buying chestnuts, try to ensure they are fresh and in good condition. Not only will they taste better, but they will also peel more easily which is no small matter.

500g carrots
1 tablespoon butter
1 small onion, chopped
3 cloves garlic
2 sprigs thyme, leaves only
120g fresh chestnuts
80g cream cheese
salt and pepper, to season

80g watercress
olive oil
200mls cream
20g Parmesan, finely grated

100cm sheet of fresh pasta, 10–12cm wide

Peel the carrots, chop them into chunks and put them into a pan with the butter, onion, garlic and thyme leaves, and enough stock or water to almost cover the carrots. Bring this to a boil, cover and simmer for 20 minutes or so until the carrots are tender. Remove the lid and boil off any liquid remaining. Put everything from the pan into a food processor and blend in short bursts to get a coarse mash.

Peel the chestnuts and boil or roast them until tender. Break or chop the cooked chestnuts into small pieces; crumble the cream cheese and stir both into the carrot. Season with salt and pepper.

Put the watercress in the food processor with a tablespoon of olive oil and blend to a smooth purée, adding a few tablespoons of water if necessary. Put the purée in a pan with the cream and Parmesan and, just before you serve the cannelloni, simmer the sauce for one minute. Season with salt and pepper.

Slice the pasta into pieces 10cm long and cook them in boiling water for a few minutes until tender. While the pasta is cooking, warm the carrot filling in a pan over low heat.

Drop the cooked pasta sheets into a bowl of cold water for a few seconds to cool them just enough to handle, then remove them to another bowl and toss them in a little olive oil. Place a few sheets on your worktop and put a heaped tablespoon of carrot filling on each. Roll the pasta around the carrot filling to form well-packed tubes. Place the filled tubes in an oven dish brushed with olive oil. Brush the tubes with more olive oil and sprinkle them with a few tablespoons of hot stock or water. Cover the dish loosely with foil and put it in the oven at 160°C/320°F, for ten minutes or so until the cannelloni are warmed through.

Heat the watercress cream. Serve the cannelloni with the watercress cream poured over.

Carrot and cabbage spring rolls with a pomegranate, mint and yoghurt sauce

First, I must admit that I changed the sauce in this recipe while reading Diana Henry's book, *Crazy Water, Pickled Lemons,* during the late stages of finishing the text of this book. Good thing it didn't come out sooner because I think, if I had read it earlier, there would have been pomegranates and all sorts of other exotic fruits, scents and flavours all over my recipes. It's a very inspiring book – if you haven't got it, go straight back to the shop and get a copy.

Carrots and cabbage are surely at the other end of the scale of exotica from pomegranates, but they make great spring rolls. Texture is equally important as taste in a spring roll, so to keep the filling crisp the vegetables are sliced very thinly and hardly cooked at all. I use the inner heart of savoy or a smooth green cabbage.

This is another recipe that needs fine big richly flavoured carrots to carry the spicing in the dish. The flavours are a variation on what I think of as North African spicing – a combination of hot, sweet and aromatic spices.

---

1 large onion

4 cloves garlic

400g carrots

100g cabbage, white or the heart of green cabbage

1 tablespoon olive oil

2 teaspoons black mustard seeds

4 bird's eye chillies, ground

1 teaspoon fennel seeds, ground

2 teaspoons cumin seeds, ground

large pinch cinnamon

large pinch nutmeg

rind of 1 orange

salt, to season

8 large spring roll pastry sheets

2 cloves garlic

1 handful mint leaves

400mls thick yoghurt

1 pomegranate

Chop the onion and garlic into very thin slices. Peel the carrots and grate them on the widest grater blade. Chop the cabbage into very thin slices.

Heat a tablespoon of olive oil in a large pan, and cook the onion and garlic for one minute. Add the spices and cook for one minute more, then add the carrot, cabbage and orange rind. Cook one more minute, stirring to combine everything, then immediately remove the pan from the heat. Season with salt.

Lay a spring roll sheet on a work surface, with a corner pointing towards you. About 4cm up from the bottom point, spread a heaped tablespoon of the filling into a 12–15cm-long shape. Fold the bottom point of the pastry over the filling and roll the pastry up tightly until just past the widest points in the middle. Fold the sides in, brush the remaining edges lightly with water and continue rolling the pastry to the end. Repeat this process with the rest of the pastry sheets.

To make the sauce, crush the garlic, chop the mint leaves and stir both into the yoghurt. Slice the pomegranate in half horizontally and use a teaspoon to scoop the seeds into a bowl. Stir four tablespoons of the seeds and their juice into the yoghurt sauce.

In a large frying pan, heat 2cm of oil to a medium temperature. Fry the spring rolls in the oil, turning once, until the pastry is crisp and lightly browned.

Serve the spring rolls with the yoghurt sauce, either as a dip or poured over the rolls.

Beetroot soup with cabbage and vodka

Big stored winter beetroots aren't best suited to roasting individually, so I tend to make them into dishes that use puréed, mashed, grated or chopped beetroot. The beetroot mousse in *The Café Paradiso Cookbook* is the one I love most, and it still greatly amuses diners in the restaurant. Beetroot also makes great risotto that looks shocking, in the best sense, and tastes wonderful. *The Paradiso Cookbook* also had a recipe for a chilled summer beetroot soup, and in a way this is a winter cousin of that recipe. Where the chilled soup had cucumber and soured cream, this robust winter version has fried cabbage and vodka for a warming kick. The vodka element I took from a beautiful meal served in the now-defunct Stepping Stone restaurant in Kerry. This was no delicate drizzle of alcohol over the soup, it was more like someone had formed a shot glass in the thick soup and poured in a generous measure of vodka – good vodka too. The effect is like having your aperitif and starter at the same time. Conversation moves along at a lively hop after that.

FOR SIX TO EIGHT:

800g beetroot

3 onions

6 cloves garlic

half a bulb of fennel or 1 stick celery

olive oil

100g potato

1500mls vegetable stock (see page 137)

1 tablespoon fresh dill, fennel or lovage

large pinch cayenne pepper

1 tablespoon balsamic vinegar

salt and pepper, to season

2 leaves savoy cabbage

vodka, to serve

cream or soured cream, to serve

Cook the beetroot in boiling water until tender, then peel under cold running water and chop coarsely.

Meanwhile, chop the onions, garlic and fennel or celery, heat some olive oil in a pot, and cook them until the onions are soft. Chop the potato and add it to the onions along with the beetroot, the stock and your chosen herb. Bring this to a boil and simmer, covered for thirty minutes or so until the potato breaks down. Add the cayenne pepper and balsamic vinegar, and simmer for one minute more. Blend the soup to a smooth purée, season well with salt and pepper, and reheat to serve.

Chop the cabbage into short, thin slices and fry them in olive oil over medium heat for a few minutes, until the cabbage is tender but not quite soft.

Pour the soup into bowls and place a little cabbage sitting in the centre on top of each. Put a teaspoon or two of vodka into each soup, in just one or two places rather than scattered thinly. Finally, if you like, drizzle a little cream or soured cream over the soup.

Potatoes

Potatoes… mmm… if I start on potatoes I might go on forever. Indeed, I wouldn't be the first. There are a few wonderful books written about potatoes, most notably *The Potato: How the Humble Spud Rescued the Western World* by Larry Zuckerman, which traces the history of the potato and the social effects of its rise from a mistrusted, potentially poisonous fodder to the staple of so many countries and cultures. He is brilliant on Ireland and the potato's role in the social structures before, during and after the famines of the nineteenth century. The potato is still a very loaded symbol in Ireland, and our relationship with it a little uneasy. Oh, we love our spuds, no doubt about that, especially those who are comfortable with being of rural stock. But we are also naturally uncomfortable with the idea of being dependent on potatoes. As a modern, wealthy and almost-civilised nation, we are pleased to have replaced potatoes with other less volatile staples like pasta. With good reason. It is well documented that the potato is a near-perfect food, capable of maintaining life for longer than any other crop. The awful irony, the awful shortcoming, of the potato as a near-perfect staple food is that it is great for only 10 or 11 months. The stress caused by the fear that the stock won't last the full year would make anyone want to liberate themselves from dependency. It's a miracle that, having loosened the potato's grip, our love for them survives. Now we eat them purely for pleasure.

The pattern of dinner in my childhood was for everyone to scoff, first, and in a cursory manner, the protein (with sauce on Fridays and Sundays), then the vegetables (carrots, turnips, parsnips and cabbage), and then to devote serious attention to the potatoes, taking first two from the piled plate in the centre of the table, followed by one more at a time, up to seven or eight, until the spuds were all gone. The condition of the protein might be acknowledged, but the potatoes would be discussed in great detail: their age, how they were holding up, their flouriness, size, dirtiness, availability and their anticipated storage life; the character of the man who dug and sold them would be admired or castigated. To this day my mother asks where I get my spuds from, never where I get the artichokes, pumpkins or asparagus.

There was only one ideal potato then: large, floury and unblemished, cheap, local and of guaranteed supply. Only rarely would we hit a vein of such perfection, of course, but the search was eternal and absorbing. Now we seem to need a lot of different potatoes, depending on whether they are to be used in mash or salads, steamed or roasted, in gratins, fried cakes or tortilla. I can't always remember the names of the ones I want. So I end up asking for things like 'some more of those fat, thin-skinned, medium-floury ones I used for tortilla last year'. It is the mark of a good wholesaler to be able to translate such vague gibberish into top-class vegetable delivery. Now then, there I am discussing the character of the potato man! Some things never change, and we become our mothers even against our steely determination.

There are so many potatoes out there at any one time – old reliables and new hybrids – and they all have their time and their dish. There is no point in trying to mash potatoes with little starch and we've all met those delicatessen potato salads made with mashing potatoes – comfort food gone too far west, I think. Until someone comes up with a scale identifying the starch content of different potatoes, we will have to go on learning by practice: the daily, weekly and seasonal routines. Try to learn about the potatoes available in your area. From what is available locally

to you, decide what is good for salad, baking, mashing and so on. Ask about variety names and remember them. All that I can do here is tell you the ones I use, but there is little point in me insisting on potato varieties you can't get. You may well already have access to perfectly good potatoes and you don't need me to tell you to switch allegiance.

I recently came across a new variety, ancient but new to me – 'pink fir apples'. I thought they were extraordinary, richly flavoured dense and heavy, yet firm in texture. Others weren't so keen, including the grower who says they're too much trouble for the yield. Almost half those who tried them said that they were "alright", an Irish euphemism for "don't do that again" – as in reply to "how was that?" "Alright".

Potato, sweet onion and basil tortilla with green chilli aioli

For tortilla, you need what the Spaniards consider a floury potato, but which is in reality about halfway on the virtual scale of flouriness, maybe a bit more. It must be just firm enough to hold its shape while frying, while leaking enough starch to make a cake of the tortilla rather than an omelette with potatoes in it. In my tiny enclave, I find Rooster and Nicola perfect for tortilla. If these names mean nothing to you, you want a potato that makes decent but slightly wet and disappointing mash – I'm sure you've come across those!

This tortilla recipe is for a very large heavy frying pan, with a 24cm base and shallow, sloped sides. It will feed six to eight people as a meal and even more as a snack or finger food. I like to serve it with some greens in tomato sauce, or the aubergine relish on page 24, but as a snack I like to eat it with aioli, all the better if it's spiced like this green chilli one. When Bridget turns up her nose at eating an egg dish with eggy sauce, I remind her of the classic egg mayonnaise, a dish that only went downhill when people started to make it from crappy eggs and cheap factory mayonnaise.

FOR FOUR:

FOR THE TORTILLA:
3 large white onions
olive oil
1kg potatoes, such as roosters or Nicola
12 eggs
large handful basil leaves
salt and pepper, to season

Chop the onions in half, then into thin slices. Heat two tablespoons of olive oil in a pan and cook the onion at a moderate temperature for half an hour or so, until it is very soft and sweet but not browned.

Meanwhile, peel the potatoes and chop them into thin chips – classic Belgian chips, that is. Heat a 2cm depth of olive oil in a large frying pan, and cook the potato chips at a fairly high temperature, stirring often to keep them separate, until the potato is cooked through and lightly coloured. At the same time, beat the eggs well, tear the basil leaves and add them to the eggs. Drain the potatoes, saving the oil to use again. Add both the potatoes and onions to the eggs while they are still hot, stirring them in quickly. This will help the egg to start cooking, making it easier to cook through to the centre of the tortilla.

Season very well with salt and pepper.

Quickly wipe the pan clean, brush it lightly with olive oil and set it over a low wide heat. Tip in the tortilla mix. Smooth down the edges quickly, then leave the tortilla to cook slowly. In ten minutes, run a spatula under the edges of the tortilla to loosen it. Slide the tortilla on to a large plate, invert the pan over it and flip it over. If you like, you can firm up the top of the tortilla a little by putting the pan under a grill before turning. Put the pan back on the heat and leave it to cook for five minutes more. The tortilla should be firm to the touch. Turn off the heat and leave the pan where it is for five minutes more.

Slide the tortilla on to a plate before cutting it into wedges. Serve it warm or at room temperature.

FOR THE AIOLI:
5 cloves garlic
1 or 2 mild fresh green chillies
1 egg
1 teaspoon smooth mustard
250mls olive oil
salt, to season
squeeze of lemon juice

Roast the garlic cloves in a low oven until soft, then squeeze the garlic from its skin. Chop the chillies and put them into a food processor with the garlic, the egg and mustard. Blend for a minute, then slowly pour in the olive oil in a thin stream, until the aioli thickens. If it becomes too thick for your liking, dilute with a few drops of hot water. Season with salt, and a squeeze of lemon juice to your taste.

Celeriac, leek and potato gratin with capers and thyme

When our family is in need of calming comfort food, Bridget cooks and I keep my advice to myself. This recipe is a variation on one of her classics: potato, leeks and garlic baked slowly in cream. Changing the focus from potatoes to celeriac makes the dish more interesting, possibly a little less like comfort food. Celeriac has a very upfront flavour, very much that of celery, as its name suggests, with a touch of the earthiness inevitable in roots. Try to buy medium-sized ones of about 600–800g. Because celeriac can be a bit gnarly, and peeling them involves slicing off the skin and roots, the smaller ones give a very poor yield; much larger celeriac can often be overblown and have a hollow centre.

Celeriac is quite a versatile root, making wonderful soup and fritters, recipes for both of which I included in *The Café Paradiso Cookbook*. The combination in this gratin recipe of potato and celeriac also makes great mash, though celeriac doesn't have enough starch to make mash on its own. The best way to make potato and celeriac mash is to make potato mash in the usual way and then to add celeriac that has been puréed in a food processor.

----

1 medium celeriac

600g potatoes (Nicola, Roosters or similar)

2 medium leeks

10 cloves garlic

3 sprigs thyme, leaves only

100mls white wine

2 tablespoons small capers

butter

salt and pepper, to season

300mls cream

Use a knife to slice the skin off the celeriac, then chop it into slices 5mm thick. Cook the slices in boiling water for three minutes. Wash the potatoes, slice them to the same thickness and cook them for three minutes too. Peel the potatoes only if the skin doesn't appeal to you.

Slice the leeks in half lengthways, wash them and chop them into slices about 2cm thick. Slice the garlic. Melt a tablespoon of butter in a pan and cook the leeks, garlic and thyme for five minutes over a fairly high heat. Pour in the wine and cook on high for one minute more. Off the heat stir in the capers.

Heat the oven to 170°C/325°F. Butter an oven dish and line the base with overlapping celeriac and potato slices. Season with salt and pepper, then cover with a thin layer of leeks, then another of celeriac and potato; repeat until the vegetables are all used up. Pour over the cream and press down gently on the vegetables. Bake for 30 to 40 minutes until the roots are tender.

Grilled potato and kale gnocchi in a hazelnut and rosemary cream

Potatoes and kale are soulmates, though usually in much more robust combinations like colcannon or soup. It wasn't my idea to somehow get kale into tiny gnocchi, it was Johan's – so I left him to figure out how to do it. He did too, bless him. The crucial part is not to overcook the kale, to preserve its flavour; and then to squeeze the living daylights out of it so that it is not bringing water to the dough, which would make it tough. After that, keep a cool head and you'll get the most refined variation of potatoes and kale ever.

As always with gnocchi, you need the most floury, starchy potato you can get, bearing in mind that the flourier the potato, the less wheat flour you will need to make a dough, and the better your gnocchi will be. In Ireland, that probably means the old reliables like Kerr's pink, queens or golden wonders.

The sauce is a basic cream sauce flavoured with the lovely warming flavours of rosemary and hazelnuts. If you can get fresh hazelnuts, it will raise the sauce to a very classy level, but quality dried hazelnuts are always very good. The sauce is lovely with pasta too, especially long fresh strands like spaghetti or linguini.

FOR FOUR:

150g hazelnuts
2 tablespoons olive oil
300mls cream
2 sprigs rosemary
2 cloves garlic

600g floury potatoes
150g kale
120g Parmesan, grated
salt and pepper, to season
120g plain white flour

Roast the hazelnuts in a moderate oven for ten minutes, then place them in a tea towel and rub them to loosen the skins. Sieve out the skin and chop the nuts finely in a food processor. Add the olive oil and blend for a few seconds to get a paste. Put the cream in a pan with the whole rosemary sprigs and cloves of garlic, and bring it to a boil. Simmer for two minutes, then leave it to infuse for 15 or 20 minutes.

Peel and steam the potatoes, then gently mash the cooked potato flesh, or pass it through a sieve. Cook the kale in boiling water for five minutes, then cool it in cold water. Squeeze out all of the water and chop the kale very finely – it is best to do this in a food processor. Stir the kale into the potato mash, add 80g of the Parmesan, and season well with salt and pepper. Add the flour and quickly work it into the potato. If the dough feels like it's not too sticky to roll out, nick off a small piece, roll it into a ball and drop it into boiling water to test. If it holds its shape firmly, without falling apart or getting gloopy on the outside, it's fine – don't add any more flour to the dough. If in any doubt, add some flour and test again. When you've got a dough you trust, tear off a piece and use your hands to roll it into a long tubular shape,

about the thickness of your finger, and cut off pieces 2–3cm long. Drop the gnocchi into a large pot of boiling water, but don't over-crowd them – do a second batch if necessary.

The gnocchi are done when they float to the top. Remove the cooked gnocchi with a slotted spoon.

While the gnocchi are cooking, take the rosemary and garlic out of the cream you prepared earlier, whisk in the hazelnut paste and gently reheat the sauce, whisking all the time. Just before you serve, whisk in the remaining 40g of Parmesan and some salt and pepper. Place the gnocchi on four small plates, or one large one, drizzle the sauce over and cook them under a hot grill for a few minutes until the sauce bubbles.

Chocolate pecan pie, whiskey ice cream and darling clementines

Few people would see this dish as being an orange one. The chocolate pecan pie will push the buttons of chocolate lovers and the whiskey ice cream will complement the pie perfectly while raising a few eyebrows; and so the clementines must be a garnish, right? I don't do garnishes, so you will have to believe me when I say that we put the dish together the other way around, adding the ice cream and the tart to create an attractive package to entice people to buy the clementines. They, after all, are the one ingredient I bought enthusiastically from a man who himself bought them because he thought they were delicious and would be a pleasure to sell; they are in the height of their season and at their juicy best. Chocolate and ice cream I can sell any day, the things that I really deal in are vegetables and fruit. There are a few people who think I did the dish just to use the corny name. As if…

Any good sweet oranges are lovely poached in this way, but around the end of December we get wonderful organic clementines, a variety of tangerine, from Spain or North Africa, very sweet and with deep-orange flesh. When serving the clementines with other accompaniments, I would often use brandy instead of whiskey. However, it is not a token thing to write 'Irish' whiskey in the recipe. Irish whiskey is very smooth and clean, mainly due to the double and triple distilling, whereas American is very sweet and decent Scottish will give your oranges a taste of the bog – not a pleasant thought.

FOR FOUR:

FOR THE PIE:

175g light muscovado sugar

150g maple syrup

3 eggs

1 egg yolk

1 tablespoon cream

half teaspoon vanilla extract

70g dark chocolate

250g pecan halves

1 pastry case, blind-baked (as in the recipe on page 56)

Gently heat the sugar and maple syrup until dissolved. Boil for two minutes, then leave it to cool a little. Beat the eggs, egg yolk, cream and vanilla gently, then beat in the syrup mixture. Melt the chocolate and stir it in.

Roughly chop two-thirds of the pecans and scatter them over the base of the prepared pastry case. Pour the custard over and arrange the remaining pecans on top. Bake at 200°C/400°F for ten minutes, then at 175°C/340°F for 30 minutes until the centre is just set. Leave the tart to cool before slicing.

FOR THE ICE CREAM:

400mls milk

5 egg yolks

125g caster sugar

2 tablespoons Irish whiskey

200mls cream

Heat the milk until almost boiling. Whisk the egg yolk and sugar until the mixture is thick and pale. Pour the milk on to the egg and sugar while still whisking, then return this custard to the pan. Heat gently, stirring, until the custard has thickened a little. Stir in the whiskey and leave the custard to cool before adding the cream and freezing in an ice cream machine.

FOR THE CLEMENTINES:

12 clementines

500g sugar

500mls water

2 cinnamon sticks

2 tablespoons Irish whiskey

Peel the clementines, slice each one into three horizontal slices and put them in a bowl.

Heat the sugar, water, cinnamon and whiskey together until boiling, then simmer for three minutes. Pour this syrup over the clementines and leave them to cool to room temperature before serving.

Baked organic pineapple with rum and spices, a lime tuille and coconut ice cream

Pineapple is an extraordinary fruit. Think about it for a minute. Try to imagine having only ever seen apples and pears, an orange once in a fancy shop, and hedge berries. Now take your first pineapple into your hands. Press it. Smell it. Slice it open. Fainted yet? It's easy to forget that extraordinariness because pineapples are always there, propping up the supermarket shelves, fresh and canned, and it pops up in the most peculiar places, like on your pizza, for god's sake! Pineapple is one of those unfortunate fruits that can't ripen by even the tiniest degree after picking, which is the second reason we have been blinded to its qualities: most pineapples in shops are very ordinary because they have been picked too soon. They can't be picked too close to ripeness for export, so the matter of when to pick becomes something of a gamble. The safe and lazy way out is to pick too soon and to hell with the flavour.

To have any hope of regaining pineapple's magic, can I suggest that you eat them only when you find one of irresistible quality? You will eat less pineapple, but enjoy it to a degree otherwise not available to you. There are three things to look, or sense, for: the skin should be predominantly orange with no green; the pineapple should give off a sweet, aromatic smell of ripeness without a hint of fermentation; the central leaves at the top should slip out easily when pulled, showing as pale yellow in colour at their base. It's a good idea to buy organic pineapples, not only for the chemical safety of it but because the people who grow organically almost always hold the final quality of the fruit as a higher priority than other producers. This is true of all foods and is probably the real reason organic food is usually so much fresher and better in flavour. It is grown to be eaten, not stacked on shelves.

Pineapple is a tropical fruit and, therefore, not really seasonal. We use it in winter to brighten up the long dark days. This recipe is almost a caricature of the flavours of the West Indies, where Columbus first came across the fruit, what with the rum, coconut and spices. Try to imagine you're lying on a beach of white sand… Okay, these things can go too far… let it go.

FOR FOUR:

FOR THE PINEAPPLE:
100mls rum
100g butter
80g dark muscovado sugar
juice of 1 lemon
half a teaspoon each cinnamon, nutmeg, ginger
1 large pineapple

Put the rum, butter, sugar, lemon and spices in a pan and heat gently until they become a bubbling syrup. Peel the pineapple and chop the flesh into large slices 2cm thick. Place them in an oven dish and pour the syrup over. Bake in an oven at 180°C/350°F for 15 minutes.

FOR THE ICE CREAM:
400mls coconut milk
100mls milk
6 egg yolks
125g sugar
125mls cream

Bring the coconut milk and milk gently to a boil. Whisk together the egg yolks and sugar until the mixture is pale and thick. Pour the milks over the egg and sugar while still whisking. Return this custard to the pan and heat gently, stirring, until the custard has thickened to coat the back of a spoon. Leave it to cool before stirring in the cream and freezing in an ice cream machine.

FOR THE TUILLE:
2 egg whites
85g caster sugar
3 tablespoons plain flour
1 tablespoon cornflour
50g melted butter
4 teaspoonfuls ground almonds
rind of 2 limes, finely grated

Beat egg whites until stiff, then beat in the sugar until glossy. Add the flour and corn-flour (through a sieve), the melted butter, almonds and lime rind. Fold gently to get a smooth, thick batter.

Line baking trays with parchment and heat an oven to 200°C/400°F. Drop teaspoonfuls of the batter on to the trays, using the back of the spoon to spread the batter into a very thin circle of 8–9cm diameter. Do just one tray at a time. Bake for four to six minutes until the tuilles are lightly coloured. Lift them from the trays carefully and drape them over a wooden spoon, an inverted cup or the side of a long glass, depending on how you want to shape them. Remember, they are very flexible, but only for a short time – in half a minute they will be crisp.

Serve a few slices of hot pineapple in their syrup, with coconut ice cream and a tuille.

Tortellini of Cashel blue cheese and sundried tomato with nutmeg spinach and an artichoke cream

Tortellini are fun to make when you get the hang of them and they give the dish an element of structure – 'height', in other words – that ravioli can't do. If it won't come together for you, serve the pasta as flat parcels, it won't taste any different.

Sometimes dishes like this can seem daunting until you break them down. Don't try to do everything in a flurry when your guests are in the hallway. Follow the example of the restaurant kitchen approach, which makes a simple job of a potentially chaotic one without compromising the quality or your sanity. The tortellini can be stored, tossed in rice flour, in the fridge for a few hours, or longer in the freezer. The sauce can be made ahead up to the point of adding cream. Then, all that's required to cook this spectacular starter is to boil the pasta, wilt some spinach and simmer a cream sauce. You can probably do that while sipping a fine sherry, holding two conversations and minding the main course in the oven. My cooks can, anyway – yak, yak, yak, all evening.

FOR FOUR:

150 Cashel blue cheese
50 sundried tomatoes, soaked
50g fine breadcrumbs
16 x 60cm sheet of fresh pasta, or equivalent

2 tinned artichokes, rinsed
2 cloves garlic
150mls vegetable stock (see page 137)
100mls white wine
400mls cream
salt and pepper, to season
1 teaspoon chopped chives

400g spinach
olive oil
salt and pepper, to season
1 large pinch grated nutmeg

Crumble the blue cheese, chop the sundried tomatoes finely and mix them with the breadcrumbs. Cut circles of 8cm from the pasta – you will need 12 for four portions but try to make a few spares to allow for accidents. Leaving an edge of 1cm, put a teaspoon of filling on one half only of each circle. Moisten the edge, fold over the empty half and press it firmly to seal the edges, making sure that you leave no air pockets inside. Holding the two unfilled corners, pull them to bring them together underneath the filled middle, which should fold away from the corners in the process. Press the corners together.

To cook the tortellini, bring a large pot of water to a boil and drop in the tortellini. Cook them at a gentle rolling boil for four or five minutes until tender.

Make the sauce when the tortellini are made but not cooked, and simmer it to thicken while the pasta cooks. Chop the artichokes and garlic, put them in a pan with the stock and wine, and simmer for five minutes. Blend to a purée in a food processor and pass the purée through a sieve. Return the purée to the pan with the cream and simmer for a few minutes until the sauce thickens to a nice pasta-coating consistency – try some on the back of a wooden spoon to get an idea. Season carefully with salt and pepper. Add the chopped chives just before you serve.

While the tortellini are cooking, wilt the spinach in a pan with some olive oil, then season it with salt and pepper and the nutmeg.

Place a little spinach on each plate and sit three or four tortellini on top. Pour some cream around.

Sweet chilli-fried tofu with leeks in coconut and lemongrass broth

Sambal oelek, the Indonesian chilli sauce, makes a great base for the marinade here because of its sweet and hot flavour, of course, but also because its slightly thickened texture helps the marinade to coat the tofu. The marinade is quite hot and, if it coats the tofu successfully, the tofu has quite a kick too, which is why I like to serve it with a cooling coconut dish.

The coconut broth is very simple, to act as a cooling foil to the hot tofu. To use it on its own as a sauce for a noodle dish, you might want to add more ginger and some other spices. As well as the coconut milk, I use a little coconut cream from one of those concentrated blocks to help thicken the broth a little. Any greens, western cabbage or Asian choi are good in the broth instead of, or with, the leeks.

If you feel the need for some carbohydrates with this, and I usually do, serve some noodles sitting underneath the leeks. Flat rice noodles are especially nice here.

FOR FOUR:

3 tablespoons sambal oelek

6 tablespoons soy sauce

2 tablespoons sugar

juice of 1 lime

600g tofu

olive oil

300mls vegetable stock (see page 137)

4 stalks lemongrass

1 tablespoon grated ginger

1 handful each basil and coriander leaves

2 medium leeks

600mls coconut milk

50g coconut cream

pinch salt

Stir together the sambal oelek, soy sauce, sugar and lime juice in a shallow bowl. Add two tablespoons of water. Chop the tofu into 12 thick slices and put them in the marinade for 15 minutes.

Heat a large frying pan and brush it with oil. Put in the tofu to fry briefly over medium heat for a minute on both sides, then pour a spoonful of marinade on to each side. Continue cooking, swirling the pan, until the marinade has been absorbed by the tofu. Turn the tofu slices once during this cooking, spooning a little more marinade over them just before the turning. You can cook the tofu in two batches and keep the first warm in an oven.

To make the coconut broth, bring the stock to a boil in a pot, drop in the lemongrass, ginger and herbs and simmer for five minutes. Remove the lemongrass and herbs. Trim the coarsest green parts from the leeks, then slice the rest into diagonal slices, wash them and put them in the stock. Simmer gently for ten minutes or so until the leeks are tender. Pour in the coconut milk, coconut cream and a pinch of salt, and simmer for one minute before serving.

Serve the tofu sitting on the leeks in a generous pool of coconut broth.

Black bean, aubergine and leek chilli with polenta gnocchi and lime soured cream

Having spent years shaking off the stodgy, wholefood associations of vegetarian food, and practically refusing to cook pulses at all except for my beloved chickpeas, I was a bit nervous about putting this simple chilli on the Paradiso lunch menu. It's been a big hit – partly, I think, because it is rich rather than heavy, and partly because we managed to make it look pretty – no mean feat with a dish that's packed with beans. The black turtle beans, small and dense, are essential to this richness, as is the aubergine. Although I vary the third vegetable in the chilli according to moods and seasons, I never cook it without aubergine. The aubergine is roasted in quite a lot of olive oil and this gives the dish a rich, oily lusciousness. Hey, I never said it was diet food! Low-fat bean stews are monotonously dull and starchy to wade through and, anyway, I don't believe that olive oil-rich food is unhealthy.

This chilli is hot. That's why it's called a chilli. Occasionally, a faint-hearted cook will leave out some of the chillies, removing the essential character of the dish. Usually by the time I find out, the cook and the bemused customers have gone home. It's a pet hate of mine: restaurant food that advertises itself as something that couldn't be detected in a blind tasting. Sometimes it's caused by meanness on the part of the kitchen or the kitchen's accountant; sometimes it's a timid belief that subtle and bland are more or less the same. If you buy something because its description includes the names of tastes you lust for but the food tastes politely of nothing, you're left with a screaming sense of frustration… or at least some mild disappointment because, well, you've become used to this happening. Chilli should taste of chilli, and if you don't like hot chillies, order a dish that doesn't include them.

The base of the chilli is a simple tomato sauce, heavily laced with the holy triumvirate of spices: chillies, cumin and coriander seeds. I don't think chilli needs a complicated spicing, but it does need a good balance. It is for simplicity and balance that I only ever use three vegetables: the beans, aubergines and one green vegetable. Any more and the dish will become too confusing to be interesting.

FOR THE CHILLI:

*200g dried black turtle
beans*

olive oil

2 onions, finely chopped

*3 cloves garlic, finely
chopped*

*1 tablespoon coriander
seeds, ground*

*1 tablespoon cumin seeds,
ground*

*8 dried bird's eye chillies,
ground*

500g tinned tomatoes

*1 tablespoon tomato
purée*

salt, to season

400g aubergines

1 large leek

1 bunch fresh coriander

Soak the turtle beans for two hours or more
in cold water, then cook them in lots of
boiling water until tender (about an hour).

Heat a little olive oil in a large pan and cook
the onions until soft. Add the garlic and
spices, and cook for two minutes before
adding the tomatoes and the tomato purée.
Bring the sauce to a boil and simmer for 15
minutes. Season with salt and check the spice
levels – the sauce needs to be very strongly
spiced at this point, as the beans and vegetables will dilute its power considerably.

While the sauce is cooking, chop the
aubergine into large chunks, toss them in
olive oil and roast them in a hot oven until
browned and softened. Turn and toss the
aubergines once or twice as they cook.

Chop the leeks into chunks and wash them.
It's best to wash unsliced leek pieces in a

large container in a few changes of water.
Heat two tablespoons of olive oil in a wide
pan and cook the leeks in it until just tender,
stirring often.

Add the cooked turtle beans, aubergines and
leeks to the sauce and simmer for ten
minutes. Stir in the fresh coriander, and
check the seasoning and spicing again before
serving.

FOR THE LIME SOURED
CREAM:

rind and juice of 1 lime

*200mls soured cream or
crème fraîche*

Stir the lime rind and juice into the soured
cream.

FOR THE GNOCCHI:

*1200mls vegetable stock
(see page 137)*

250g coarse maize

1 teaspoon salt

60g cream cheese

*1 tablespoon chives, finely
chopped*

Bring the stock to a boil in a large pot, then
whisk in the maize and the salt over high
heat until the stock comes back to the boil,
then quickly turn the heat to a very low
setting and replace the whisk with a wooden
spoon. Cook the polenta for 15 to 20
minutes, stirring frequently, until the grains
are soft. Stir in the cream cheese and chives,
and tip the polenta out on to an oiled tray.
Try to keep the polenta at a height of about
2cm, which may mean not using the full tray
to spread the wet polenta on. Spread the
polenta evenly and quickly, using your hands
dampened with cold water or a spatula. In
about 20 minutes, the polenta will be ready
to cut, but leave it longer if you can. (In fact,
the polenta can be made up to a day in
advance.) Use a circular cutter to cut small
circles from the polenta. About five minutes

before serving, toss the polenta pieces in
olive oil and roast them in a hot oven until
crisped on the outside

Serve the chilli surrounded by some of the
polenta gnocchi and soured cream.

Rigatoni with winter greens, artichokes, dried tomatoes, chillies and capers

This combination of cupboard ingredients and fresh winter vegetables sounds like a mouthful to say, never mind to eat, but it's just pasta and vegetables with two strong flavours I use together a lot at home – chillies and capers. Put this on a restaurant menu and half the people who order it will ask for one or more of these ingredients to be left out. At home, you can do the same to adjust the dish to your likes and dislikes, and without upsetting any fragile cheffy egos.

Kale and cabbage are surprisingly good in pasta, though they do cook differently. Kale, and smoother cabbages and spring greens, will cook down to a softly chewy finish while tougher cabbages like savoy will hold their essential character more, but in a way that is completely compatible with the strong flavours of this dish.

FOR FOUR:

1 small leek
200g kale or cabbage
6 large tinned artichokes
500g rigatoni
3 tablespoons olive oil
3 cloves garlic, thinly sliced
8 halves of sundried tomatoes, thinly sliced
4 dried bird's eye chillies, chopped
1 tablespoon small capers
pinch salt
Parmesan, finely grated, to serve

Halve the leek lengthways, wash and chop it into thin diagonal slices. Chop the greens into similar slices. Drain the artichokes and rinse them very well under lots of running cold water.

Bring a pot of water to a boil and cook the rigatoni until just tender.

At the same time, heat three tablespoons of olive oil in a pan, and cook the leeks and greens together for five minutes, then add the garlic, artichokes, dried tomatoes and chillies. Cook for a few minutes more until the cabbage is tender, then add the capers and a pinch of salt.

Drain the pasta and stir it into the vegetables. Serve with some finely grated Parmesan to sprinkle over.

Pistachio, cardamom and basmati rice cake with coconut greens and gingered mango salsa

Although this recipe gives instructions for cooking basmati rice, this is more of a recipe for leftover rice, or at least rice cooked much earlier on in the day. It could be seen as a way to serve rice and greens in a pretty and structured way in a restaurant, but there is more than aesthetics to it. As much as the shaping into a cake is for appearance, it also gives a texture that is vastly different from scooping up a plate of rice. There should be just enough egg in the mix to hold the cake together without making a too-solid mass. The dish is very fine in itself but will find a perfect balance if you also serve a simple tomato-based curry of green beans, squash or broccoli.

In her beautiful book *Crazy Water, Pickled Lemons,* Diana Henry says there should always seem to be just too little cardamom, leaving an element of tease. This was a revelation to me, so I checked this and some other cardamom recipes to see if I was hitting people over the head where I might have been better off teasing. Let's just say, I'll be saving some money on the cardamom seeds in future.

FOR FOUR:

olive oil
250g basmati rice
250mls boiling water
large pinch salt
60g pistachio nuts
8 cardamom pods
1 small leek, white part only
butter
2 eggs

half a mango
1 sweet ginger nut in syrup
juice of 1 lime

1 red onion
kale, spinach or green cabbage
400mls coconut milk

Heat a little oil in a pan and gently toast the basmati in it for a few minutes, then pour in the boiling water and a large pinch of salt. Simmer, covered, over very low heat for ten minutes, then turn off the heat and leave the pan for five minutes. Turn the rice out into a wide bowl and leave it to cool.

Toast the pistachios lightly in an oven, then chop them coarsely. Crack the cardamom pods, remove the seeds and discard the pods. Chop the leek finely. Melt a little butter in a pan and cook the leek, pistachio and cardamom for two minutes, then stir this into the rice. When the rice is cool, or just before you cook the cakes, stir in the eggs.

Dice the mango flesh and the ginger, and stir them together with the lime juice and a teaspoon of the ginger syrup.

Heat four rings 10cm in diameter by 2cm high in a wide shallow pan over low heat, brush them lightly with olive oil and fill them with the rice mix, pressing it in to get an even finish. Cook the cakes for five minutes before flipping them over to cook the other sides. Cook until both sides are lightly coloured and the cakes are just set. If you don't have a pan big enough to hold all four, the cooked cakes will keep warm in a low oven while you do a second batch.

As the cakes are cooking, slice the red onion thinly and tear the greens. Cook them together in a little olive oil over high heat until the greens are wilted, then pour in the coconut milk and take the pan off the heat.

Serve each rice cake sitting on some greens, with a little dollop of mango salsa on top.

Tagliolini with lemon, olive oil, chickpeas, flat leaf parsley and pecorino

Bridget made this one evening when we were huddled in front of the television watching a video. We were tired, in need of a family night in with the curtains drawn and a fire in the grate. Maybe I should lie and say it was a winter's evening, but the truth is that it was in the early stages of that dreadful summer of rain, and the dish came about for the not very seasonal reason that the cupboard was bare, as were the fridge and pantry. Like the cobbler's barefoot children, I'm afraid a professional cook's pantry is often a neglected thing. Well, it wasn't quite bare, because Bridget knocked up this simple but stunning combination. It distracted me from the plot of the movie and my ranting about the perfect simplicity and simple perfection of the meal distracted everyone else to the point that we abandoned the telly for a friendly but vicious game of cards. The power of food, eh?

The whole thing can be cooked in less time than the argument about whose turn it is to cook, especially if you have fresh pasta to hand and you use tinned chickpeas. It is my natural inclination to meddle with recipes, add a few more ingredients, make things a little more complex, sometimes just keeping one element and ending up with another dish entirely. So I have thought of altering this, and I do believe it will stand a little meddling and personalising, but I decided to write down the classic version and let the rest of you get on with your own meddling. Some things that would definitely work would be the addition of garlic and/or chillies, using rocket instead of parsley or tinned artichokes instead of chickpeas. Always, when confronted by something new, whether a dish or a vegetable, it's best to try it straight first and then the possibilities will open up.

I have suggested pecorino, a hard sheep's cheese, here because the dish seems to have a southern Italian or eastern Mediterranean character, and sheep's cheese fits into that picture. However, if you can't get, or don't like, sheep's cheese, then Parmesan or any hard cheese will be fine.

FOR FOUR:

120mls olive oil

rind of 2 lemons

juice of half a lemon

200g cooked chickpeas

large handful flat leaf parsley

500g fresh tagliolini pasta, or similar

salt and black pepper, to season

100g pecorino or other hard cheese, finely grated

Put the olive oil, lemon rind and juice and chickpeas into a pan large enough to hold the cooked pasta. Tear the parsley leaves from their stalks and finely chop any stalk tender enough to use, then add the parsley to the pan.

Bring a pot of water to a boil and drop in the pasta to cook for two or three minutes until just tender. While the pasta is cooking, cook the sauce ingredients over a medium heat for two minutes. Drain the pasta and stir it into the sauce with a generous seasoning of salt and black pepper, and half of the grated cheese. Serve the pasta with more cheese scattered over.

Braised cannellini beans

Variations on this bean dish have become a staple on Paradiso menus since I first made it a few years back. As well as its primary function as an intensely flavoured accompaniment to many dishes such as the cabbage dolma on page 209, gratins, crêpes and so on, it is a good base for a stew or pasta dish.

The beans are cooked in two stages: first in water and then in the sauce in the oven. Be careful to get them out of the water before they are fully cooked or they will turn to mush in the second cooking.

Don't think of all dried beans as the same – as with any product, it is worth buying from someone who you know buys good produce and has a good turnover of stock. Age is a crucial factor in beans. Dried beans should be from the previous harvest or, at worst, the one before, but there are beans on the market much older than that. Usually you can tell by the skin – any wrinkling or discolouring is a dead giveaway, but check the 'use by' date too.

FOR FOUR:

400g dried cannellini beans
150mls olive oil
150mls white wine
200mls vegetable stock (see page 137)
3 sprigs thyme
1 sprig rosemary
4 cloves garlic
4 sundried tomatoes
salt and pepper, to season

Soak the beans in cold water for at least two hours, then cook them in boiling water for 30 to 60 minutes, depending on their age and quality, until the beans are almost but not quite tender. Strain the beans and put them back in the pot with the olive oil, wine, stock, thyme and rosemary. Slice the garlic thinly and chop the sundried tomatoes into small dice, then stir both into the beans. Season with salt and pepper. Bring the beans to a boil and transfer them to an oven dish. Cover the dish loosely with a sheet of baking parchment and place it in the oven, at 180°C/350°F. Check the beans after half an hour, and every 20 minutes or so after that. You may need to add some more liquid. The beans should be cooked after an hour but it may take longer, and remember that the longer and slower the cooking the more the beans will have absorbed the flavours around them. When done, the beans will be tender and the liquids will have come together and reduced to a moist, well-flavoured background sauce.

Blood orange and fennel sorbet with marinated blood oranges

We get organic blood oranges from Sicily late in winter, just as spring is about to, well, spring. They're not exactly a sign of spring, but you know you're almost there and that, before the oranges are all gone, there will be greens sprouting furiously. At the creeping onset of every winter I have a sense of dread about the vegetables we gradually lose as we go deeper into the cold season. Coming out the other end, the excitement of the new year ahead is always accompanied by a sense of reassessment, and I think that, yeah, that wasn't so bad, we had some nice food in there, in the deep dark recesses; it always turns out okay and winter has its own enjoyable challenges. Then I pull myself together, shut the winter away and get on with the good things in life. As a last throw of the season, blood oranges are a class act and certainly no novelty. At their best, they have a very fine, intense flavour, as perfectly balanced between sweet and acid as an orange gets. We poach them and serve them with puddings and cheesecakes, or with a sorbet of the same flavours, as here. The aniseedy flavour of fennel is excellent with oranges, in savoury cooking as in desserts. Make a decent batch of sorbet and before it's gone there will be daffodils in the garden.

FOR FOUR:

750g caster sugar
450mls water
handful of fennel herb
12 large blood oranges
1 egg white

Make a fennel syrup by bringing the sugar, water and fennel to a boil; simmer for five minutes and leave to cool for an hour. Grate the rind of six blood oranges finely, squeeze the juice from them and add them to 600mls of the syrup. Whisk the egg white briefly, fold it into the syrup and freeze in an ice cream machine.

Peel the remaining oranges with a knife, slicing off the skin and the outer white pith. Slice each orange horizontally into three or four thick slices. Heat the remaining syrup to just below boiling, pour it over the oranges and leave to cool.

Serve the sorbet with some marinated blood oranges.

Early Spring

spring greens

purple sprouting
broccoli

watercress

Spring cabbage timbale of roasted aubergine and Gabriel cheese with a plum tomato-basil sauce

The outer leaves of spring cabbage are soft, dark and very supple when cooked, and they make a wonderful material for parcels of all sorts. In this recipe the inside leaves of the cabbage form the bulk of the parcel filling too. So in a way the cabbage is put back together, though in a very formal reconstruction and not at all in a way that its mammy would recognise. Although there is a bit of fiddly preparation and construction involved in these timbales, it is quite rewarding if you like that kind of work. Also, the construction is very solid, more packing than delicate arrangement, and there are no tricky cooking techniques involved at all. You will, however, need individual metal rings to hold the timbales together as they cook in the oven. The fundamental idea of the dish – constructing a drum-like timbale from cabbage leaves – will accommodate a wide range of variations on the filling, whether they use the inner cabbage leaves or not. This is the first version I did, and I'm still very fond of it. Okay, it's not the most certifiably seasonal version of the timbale, but equally it's important not to get too hung up on absolutes when dealing with food – down that road lies nothing but paranoia and self-flagellation. When I did the timbale without the aubergines, it missed them more than I could bear. Equally, the plum tomato sauce I originally used, and include here, is out of season unless you use tinned tomatoes (and they would do very nicely if you drain them carefully), but it's just so perfect… Serve the timbales with some steamed or roast potato. Later in the season some grilled asparagus will give the dish a luxurious finish.

FOR FOUR:

4 plum tomatoes
1 bunch basil leaves
150mls olive oil
salt and pepper, to season
2 heads spring cabbage
1 leek, chopped
4 cloves garlic, chopped
100g Gabriel cheese
1 small bunch chives
2 aubergines
splash of water or stock

The tomato sauce can be prepared at any time during the timbale preparation. Cut a little cross into the base of the tomatoes and drop them into boiling water for a few seconds. Remove the tomatoes to cold water and peel off the skins. Cut the tomatoes in half and scoop out the seeds. Chop the flesh into dice. Put the basil in a jug with the olive oil and use a hand blender to make a basil oil. Put the tomatoes in a small pan with enough of the oil to give a wet consistency. Season with salt and pepper. When you are ready to serve the timbales, heat the sauce for one minute.

Separate the outer leaves from the cabbage heads. You will need one or two leaves per portion, depending on their size. Trim any thick stalk to the thickness of the leaf. Bring a pot of water to a boil, drop in the leaves and cook them until tender, about five minutes. Lift the leaves out of the pot and put them in a bowl of cold water to stop the cooking. Wash the leek, slice it in half lengthways and chop it into thin slices. Chop the remaining cabbage in the same way and mix it with the leek and the garlic. Heat some oil in a wide pan and cook the cabbage and leek until just

beginning to soften. Move it to a bowl to cool, then stir in the cheese and the chives. Season with a little salt and pepper.

Cut the aubergine into rounds of 1cm thickness, brush them with olive oil on both sides and roast them in a hot oven, 200°C/400°F, until browned and fully cooked.

Take a metal ring of 7 or 8cm diameter. Brush the inside lightly with olive oil and push a cabbage leaf into the ring, ideally to cover over half of the base, half of the side and with some leaf overhanging. It may take one more leaf, or two to three leaves or pieces of leaves, to give a full single-layer covering of the base and the sides, each piece overhanging the top of the ring. Cover the base with a layer of aubergine slices, then a thick layer of the cabbage and cheese mix, to just short of the top, followed by another layer of aubergine slices. Fold over the overhanging cabbage leaves and trim them so that they cover the top adequately but not too thickly. Brush the top with olive oil. Repeat the process to get four timbales. Place the timbales in an oven dish brushed with olive oil and sprinkle a little stock or water over them. Cook the timbales in an oven at 180°C/350°F, sprinkling a little water over occasionally to stop the timbales drying out or the cabbage burning. After ten minutes, flip over the timbales to cook both sides evenly, and cook them for a further five minutes.

Serve the timbales sitting in a pool of the tomato-basil sauce, with some grilled asparagus spears and steamed potato.

Braised spring cabbage and tomato pesto rolls

All cabbages seem to love the sweetness of tomatoes, and the lovely fresh cabbage of early spring is no different, though locating a nice sweet tomato in early spring can be tricky. Which is why, in winter and spring, I often use dried tomatoes or roasted tomatoes from the freezer. These little stubby cabbage rolls are an attempt to dress the first greens of the year up for dinner but without over-elaborating or making the filling the focus. Served in their juice, they are fantastic with a rich risotto, say with blue cheese and spring onions or wild garlic, or they can help to make a fine dinner of a simple potato gratin. In the Paradiso kitchen, they are a good-humoured pick-me-up for flagging cooks.

FOR FOUR:

2 tablespoons pinenuts

3 tablespoons thick tomato pesto

1 head spring cabbage

olive oil

200–300mls vegetable stock (see page 137)

Lightly toast the pinenuts in a heavy pan over low heat, or on a tray in the oven, until very lightly coloured. Tip them on to a chopping board and chop them roughly with a knife, then stir them into the tomato pesto.

Cut the base off the cabbage and separate the leaves. Bring a pot of water to a boil, drop in the leaves, giving the dark outer ones a head start of a minute or two, and cook them until tender, about six to eight minutes. Remove the leaves to a bowl of cold water to stop the cooking while preserving their lovely colour. Lay the leaves flat on a work surface and spread a thin layer of the pinenuts in pesto on each one. Fold a third of a large leaf over on itself, then fold again. Starting at a short end, roll the leaf, reasonably tightly but not so the

pesto squirts out. You should have something that resembles a green cigar stub. Repeat this with the rest of the leaves, bearing in mind that smaller leaves will possibly take just one initial fold. Cut the larger stubs in half but leave the smaller ones – an inch (3mm) is a nice size. Place them in a small oven dish, brush them generously with a good olive oil and spoon over enough stock to just cover the bottom of the dish. Place the dish in a moderate oven, about 180°c/350°f, for 12 to 15 minutes. Ideally the oils from the brushing and the pesto will have mingled perfectly with the stock to give a sweet rich gravy to serve the rolls in.

Spring greens and potato colcannon

You can make colcannon out of potato and greens at any time of year, so this version differs from a winter one only in the taste of the greens. But if you accept, as I do, that the fresh greens of a season offer its most defining flavours, then this colcannon will be as different to a winter one made with kale or savoy cabbage as a miserable, cold and wet day in early December is to a bright, slightly-chilly-but-getting-there day in early March. Spring cabbage, fast-growing, soft and bursting with life, tastes of its time, and indeed even bringing it home from the market instead of that hoary old, frostbitten last-of-the-winter cabbage can put a spring in your step and make the year seem full of promise. Honest.

FOR FOUR:

1 kg floury potatoes
half head spring cabbage
4 spring onions, chopped finely
4 cloves garlic, chopped finely
2 tablespoons olive oil
200mls milk
60g butter
salt and pepper, to season

Peel the potatoes and steam them until soft. Chop the cabbage and cook it in boiling water until tender, then drain and chop it quite finely. Fry the onion and garlic in the olive oil for two minutes. Add the cabbage and cook for one minute more. Warm the milk and butter together in a large pot, then add the potatoes and mash them until you have a smooth mash. Nothing will cause more derision in an Irish household, even in the twenty-first century, than lumpy mash, so do go at it with some energy, but don't ever be tempted to put it in the blender – that's called thick soup. Stir in the cabbage and season well with salt and black pepper, though white pepper would be more, strictly traditionally, correct.

Spring greens with coriander seeds, chillies and ginger

A simple fried cabbage recipe that I use as a side dish to liven up many dinners at home. If dinner is in the child-friendly and comfort-food zone, a side dish with a little fire and the freshness of greens is a nice option. Ginger, chilli and coriander are all great cabbage spices, separately or together, but the coriander seeds shine here, the cracked seeds bursting with aromatic flavour. At least they do if you buy fresh seeds in good condition. It really is important with dried spices to hunt down a good source, and an organic one too if you can.

FOR FOUR:

1 head spring cabbage
4 spring onions
2 teaspoons coriander seeds
1 fresh chilli, sliced
olive oil
2 teaspoons fresh ginger, grated
2 tomatoes, sliced
1 teaspoon soy sauce

Cut the base off the cabbage and slice the leaves in half lengthways, then across in pieces about 1mm wide. Trim the spring onions and slice them diagonally in long pieces. Crush the coriander seeds with the back of a knife or a rolling pin – they should split or just open.

Heat some olive oil in a wok or wide pan and toss in the cabbage. Cook over a medium heat for a minute, then add the spring onions and the spices. Fry for another few minutes, stirring and turning the cabbage constantly, until the cabbage is tender. Finally, add the sliced tomato and the soy sauce, and heat through for one minute more.

Warm salad of purple sprouting broccoli with radishes, Parmesan polenta and avocado oil

Purple sprouting broccoli is often the first local fresh greens we get after the long winter up to our elbows in roots – not that I don't love my roots too, but I do drop them like discarded peelings when the ground thaws and something beautiful and green pushes its head up. Sprouting broccoli has a shortish season, but if you can convince different growers to grow early and late crops it can stretch for up to eight weeks, thus carrying you through from late winter to the end of spring. It still hasn't made an impact in the shops, and seems to be grown only by dedicated growers who appreciate it for itself. Although there are some interesting hybrids of broccoli with thinner, tender stalks appearing in supermarkets, they don't come near the real thing for taste. I have come to accept that the only way sprouting broccoli will become more widely available is for the public and producers alike to accept that it is a luxury vegetable with a market value similar to, say, asparagus.

If you grow your own, you know how to prepare it. If you are lucky to have access to it in a farmers' market, it should be sold more or less in a ready-to-use state – thin, single shoots about three to four inches long, the edible leaves attached. The most you should have to do is trim a little off the ends. Any sprouting broccoli sold in heads will have up to 80 per cent waste by weight, and should have an appropriately lower price.

This recipe is really a loose sketch, a prototype of endless variations, the essence of which is some purple sprouting broccoli wilted in good olive oil and served at room temperature with a little carbohydrate, polenta, crostini, potato maybe. Without the carbs, it can just as easily be a side dish, part of a main course or a little something to suck on just because you feel like it. Sprouting broccoli seems to give as much to olive oil in the cooking as it takes from it, and, to be honest, I rarely cook it any other way .

The only decent avocado oil I have ever found is from New Zealand, where avocado cultivation has been perfected – it is just appearing outside New Zealand as I write, and if it hasn't found its way into every foodie home by publication date I'll… I'll… well, I'll sell my shares.

FOR FOUR:

1 litre vegetable stock (see page 137)

200g coarse maize

1 teaspoon salt

60g Parmesan grated

2 tablespoons parsley, finely chopped

black pepper, to season

2 tablespoons avocado oil

4 handfuls sprouting broccoli

splash of water or stock

1 small red onion, thinly sliced

1 bunch radishes, thickly sliced

First make the polenta. Bring the stock to a boil in a large pot, then whisk in the maize and the salt, whisking over high heat until the stock comes back to the boil, then quickly turn the heat to a very low setting and replace the whisk with a wooden spoon. Cook the polenta for about 20 minutes, stirring frequently, until the grains are soft. Stir in the Parmesan, herbs and a generous sprinkling of black pepper, then tip the polenta out on to a work surface or into an oiled tray – a tray or dish about 25cm square will give a good thickness of polenta, but a little thinner is fine; using an open work surface will give the polenta that rustic cooking feeling you may very well be after. Either way, spread the polenta evenly and quickly, using your hands dampened with cold water or a spatula. Work quickly – the polenta sets fast. In about 20 minutes, it will be ready to cut, but leave it longer if you can. In fact the polenta can be made up to a day in advance.

Cut the polenta into small wedges. Heat a grill, lightly brush the wedges with olive oil and place them under the grill on a tray, turning once to brown both sides. Or you can cook them in the same way on a griddle pan.

At the same time, heat one tablespoon of avocado oil in a pan and toss in the sprouting broccoli. Cook it over a medium to high heat for about five or six minutes, turning and stirring almost constantly, and occasionally splashing in a little stock to keep the broccoli wilting and stop it from frying. Add the red onion slices and cook for one minute more, and then stir in the radish slices to heat through.

Pile the salad on to plates, tuck the freshly grilled polenta wedges in under the salad, and drizzle some avocado oil hither and thither.

Purple sprouting broccoli with dried tomatoes and garlic on a corn pancake of leeks and puy lentils, with a rosemary cream

It surprised me when I sat down to write out this recipe that it seems an elaborate dish of many parts and much labour. In the restaurant, it seems a simple one – some briefly cooked vegetables on a simple pancake – and with elements of it being made by different people at different times, it doesn't seem much trouble to any particular person in the process, especially the one who finishes it by cooking the broccoli and the sauce: me. The thing is that I really wanted to make an impressive main course with the sprouting broccoli, but everything I looked at that involved lots of cooking, chopping or processing of the vegetable, only reminded me that, although it can deal with many flavours, strong and robust ones too, the broccoli itself is always best left whole and briefly cooked. So, how to make an impressive main course out of that? In a sense, I just plonked it on top of what is already a main course looking for a vegetable, and inverted the way it might read on the menu. I don't mean that to seem devious, rather that what I want to get across is that the star element of the dish, the part I want the customer to be attracted to, is the purple sprouting broccoli. The dishes I focus most attention on in Paradiso are the ones that are designed to draw attention to a particular vegetable in the prime of its season, and even if there are more expensive elements in the dish, or more intensely flavoured ones, they are subordinate, present only to enhance and support the star vegetable and the customers' pleasure in it.

The quantities in the pancake recipe are tiny – it will make five pancakes if you're good and have no accidents. I would suggest that, for peace of mind, you make a double batch and have the spares for breakfast tomorrow.

FOR FIVE:

FOR THE PANCAKES:

50g fine cornmeal

20g plain flour

large pinch each paprika and turmeric

quarter teaspoon salt

1 egg

140mls milk

50g puy lentils

800g leeks

olive oil

2 cloves garlic, finely chopped

1 teaspoon Dijon mustard or similar

small sprig thyme

50mls white wine

100mls cream

salt and pepper, to season

50g Gabriel or other hard cheese, finely grated

Sift the flours and seasonings together. Whisk the egg with the milk, then whisk this into the flour mix. Use this batter to make thin pancakes, taking care to whisk up the batter each time, as the corn tends to sink, causing the pancakes to stick.

Cook the lentils in boiling water until just tender, then drain them.

Slice the leeks in half lengthways, wash them well, then chop the lengths across into short slices. Heat a pan, large enough to hold the leeks, to a high temperature, pour in a little olive oil and immediately toss in the leeks and garlic. Cook on high heat, stirring often, until the leeks soften. Add in the mustard, thyme and white wine, cook for one minute, then add the cream. Keep the heat high, boiling the cream and, hopefully, reducing the liquid from the leeks, to give a dryish, creamy finish. If you end up with a very wet mixture at this point, don't keep boiling to evaporate the liquid or you will overcook the leeks. Instead, drain the leeks, saving the liquid, then reduce the liquid on its own and pour it back into the leeks. Finally, stir in the lentils and season with salt and pepper.

Lay a pancake on the bench, prettiest side down. Place a rectangular thin layer of the leek and lentils in the centre of the pancake, sprinkle a little cheese over it, then fold up the rest of the pancake, short sides first, then the long sides, to form a closed parcel, and brush the top with olive oil. When you need to cook the pancakes, they need 10 to 15 minutes in a moderate oven, 180–190°C/350–375°F.

FOR THE ROSEMARY CREAM:

100mls vegetable stock (see page 137)

200mls cream

50mls rosemary oil

large pinch Gabriel cheese or similar

Bring the stock to a boil in a small pan and simmer until there is just a tablespoon left. Add the cream and simmer again for two minutes, then whisk in the rosemary oil and cheese. Season lightly. The sauce should really be made at the last minute but, if you're anxious, you can get it done a little before and add a splash of stock or water before heating it through to serve.

FOR THE BROCCOLI:

4 handfuls purple sprouting broccoli

6 cloves garlic

100g semi-sundried tomatoes

Heat some of the rosemary oil in a wide pan, toss in the broccoli and cook over a fairly high heat, stirring constantly for two minutes. Add in the garlic and the tomatoes, and continue cooking for a further three to four minutes, adding an occasional splash of stock or water to prevent burning or sticking. In any case, finish with a splash of stock before removing from the heat so that the dish finishes just a little moist with juice.

To serve, place a pancake on each plate (check the bottom side, sometimes it's better-looking and always a flatter surface). Pile a mound of broccoli and tomatoes on top and pour the rosemary cream around. Finish with some small, peeled and steamed potatoes dotted around in the cream.

Stir-fried sprouting broccoli, carrots and almonds in a hot-and-sour black bean sauce

Despite my fondness for sprouting broccoli with olive oil, the vegetable has more than enough character to be used with Asian-style flavourings, whether simply seasoned with ginger and sesame oil or with this very robust sauce. I've been using this sauce since the early days of Café Paradiso, and I would guess that, for everyone who gets a kick out of it, there's another who finds it shocking. Come to think of it, I haven't used it at all this past year – hope I'm not losing my nerve. Maybe it's the staff – for all their fine qualities of subtlety and finesse, I do find it a bit tricky working with cooks who don't like chilli – everyone's insecure to some extent and having someone go 'oh, yeucch' or roaring in pain behind you will wear you down eventually. The sauce is very hot and quite sour, but a little goes a long way, and it is great fun to eat if you're into those things, certainly more than its Chinese restaurant cousin, the 'sweet and sour', which is usually more one than the other and not a lot of anything. Serve this with noodles or rice, though be warned that rice will absorb the sauce more than noodles.

The recipe for the sauce will make more than you need at one time. It is impossible to make smaller quantities than these; so, if you get to like it, I suggest you make a bigger quantity, as it keeps for a week or more in a sealed jar in the fridge.

FOR FOUR:

75g salted black beans

4 cloves garlic, finely chopped

1 tablespoon ginger, grated

1 teaspoon dried chillies, ground

250mls hot water

100mls rice or white wine vinegar

25mls sherry or sake

25mls soy sauce

1 teaspoon sugar

PER PERSON, TO STIR FRY:

half a small onion, thinly sliced

1 handful purple sprouting broccoli

2 baby carrots, halved, or 1 medium carrot, sliced

1 dessertspoon sliced almonds, lightly toasted

Put half of the salted beans in a food processor with the garlic, ginger and chillies and pulse them to get a very coarse mash. Transfer this to a jug, add the rest of the beans, the liquids and the sugar, and leave for two hours to soak. Taste a little of this sauce before you use it, so you know what you're dealing with. Remember that it will be merely coating the vegetables, but also that while the sauce is not thickened it will be reduced and intensified in the pan.

Heat some oil to a fairly high temperature in a wok, and drop in the onion, broccoli and carrots together. Cook over a high heat, stirring all the time, occasionally splashing in some water to add a little steam to the process, but not so much that it slows the cooking. Just as you sense the vegetables are almost done, no more than five minutes, add a ladle of the black bean sauce – try 50mls per person the first time and adjust that to your taste next time – and cook for a further minute at high heat to boil off some of the liquid. Add the almonds just before serving.

Goats' cheese crottin and caramelised red onion in a hazelnut tartlet with watercress pesto

The first batch of watercress arrives. You feel, or imagine, just a hint of warmth in the air, and it seems like a good time to lighten the food a little. Watercress has a vibrant, peppery flavour that adds sparkle to salads and makes great sauces and soups. Watercress pesto retains the peppery sharpness of the raw leaves and is a fantastic sauce for pasta or eggs. The flavour does fade, however, so use it within two days to get the best out of it.

Crottins, the miniature whole cheeses of goats' milk, are used in these little tartlets in preference to using, say, a slice of a large log of goats' cheese. The very youngest crottins are essentially tiny logs of fresh cheese, but they mature very quickly as the surface mould grows all round the relatively small surface. Thus a crottin that is about two weeks' old is perfect here, as it will have a thin skin to help it keep its shape in the pastry case, but will still have that mild, fresh flavour that is in keeping with spring cheeses. You can, of course, get more mature crottins with a thick skin and intense flavour. If that's your thing, go right ahead; they make a fine snack with crackers and a hearty bottle of red, but don't use them in these delicate little tartlets.

FOR SIX TARTLETS:

40g hazelnuts
150g plain flour
large pinch of salt
75g cold butter
40mls cold water

400g red onions
4 tablespoons brown sugar
4 tablespoons balsamic vinegar

140g watercress
1 clove garlic
40g walnuts
200–250mls olive oil
40g Parmesan, finely grated
3 goats' cheese crottins, 80g each

If you can get good-quality blanched hazelnuts… well, lucky you. Otherwise, roast the hazelnuts for about 20 minutes in a low to medium oven, then remove their skins by wrapping the nuts in a towel or cloth and rubbing them. Grind the skinned hazelnuts as finely as possible, then sift them with the flour and salt. Cut in the butter. A food processor does this very efficiently, but remove the pastry to a bowl before stirring in the water with a few quick strokes. Shape the pastry into a ball with your hands, flatten it gently and chill for at least half an hour. Roll the pastry and cut out circles to fit six small tartlet cases of about 7cm diameter. Prick the pastry cases all over with a fork and chill them again for 30 minutes; then bake them for eight to ten minutes at 180°C/350°F until crisp. Check after five minutes in case the pastry has puffed up in places; if it has, press it gently back in place while it is still soft. Slice the red onions in half, then into thin slices. Cook the onion in a little olive oil, stirring often, until the onions are fully cooked and beginning to caramelise. Add the sugar and balsamic vinegar, and continue to cook for a further 20 minutes or so until the onions are very soft and the liquid is syrupy. Leave to cool.

Put 100g of the watercress, the garlic and walnuts in a food processor and chop to a coarse purée. Add 200mls of olive oil and blend briefly to get a thick sauce. Add more oil if the pesto seems too thick, then stir in the Parmesan. Check the seasoning, and add salt and pepper if needed.

Put a tablespoon of caramelised red onion in each pastry case. Cut the crottins in half across the centre and place a half in each pastry case, skin side up. Bake the tartlets at 190°C/375°F until heated through, and the cheese has coloured a little and started to melt. Chop the remaining watercress coarsely and serve the tartlets sitting on a little of it, with the watercress pesto spooned around.

Grilled watercress and potato gnocchi with wild garlic and a roasted tomato cream

My neighbours, and anyone else who calls round, will tell you that I'm not the most enthusiastic gardener. I can dig a hole if Bridget points me at the spot, and I'm quite good at chopping down an unloved, oversized bush that has decided to become a tree in late life. There are two plants I guard carefully, however. One is the lemon verbena that wafts an incredible scent around the back door and gives a strong hint of childhood sherbet to desserts in Paradiso. The other is the white-flowered grass-like cousin of bluebells that we call wild garlic. During the early growth of spring, no mowing is allowed anywhere near it, and this year it is halfway across the 'lawn' because Bridget is away in New Zealand testing the sea temperatures in the Bay of Plenty. I am told by one who affects to know these things that what I have is a wild leek, and another similar plant with a wider leaf has been produced to make mine feel like a counterfeit. Both plants are hedge dwellers, the flowers of both are as edible as the stems, and both spread merrily if encouraged – so if you can get hold of either, give it a home at the base of your hedge or fence and don't mow quite so close to the edge in the spring. Some very finely sliced young spring onions and/or chives will be just lovely in this recipe while you wait for next spring to come round.

If you want to learn more about the hundreds of plants known as wild garlic, check out Alan Davidson's *Oxford Companion to Food*; in fact if you want to find out anything about anything, get a copy. My current favourite item in the book is the disgusting sea cucumber and the worm that lives off its, er, delicacies – look it up for the full horror. And no, it's not a vegetable.

The weights and measurements in this recipe need to be taken as guidelines only. So much depends on the flouriness of the potatoes you use, and the moisture content of the cress. You simply have to do it, get a feel for it, and do it often enough not to forget what that feels like. That might only be a few times a year if you have a good tactile memory. When these, or any other gnocchi, are on the menu in Paradiso, one person is put in charge of making it for the time it stays on the menu. Once they get it right and know what 'right' feels like, the small adjustments caused by potato types and so on are a doddle to adapt to. What you are trying to achieve is this: get a good balance of potato and watercress, lots of cress, in a lightish, soft dough, and flavour it very well with Parmesan, salt and pepper. The potato will give a nice soft texture to the gnocchi but won't quite hold it together. So you add flour to help make a dough. The wetter your potato, the more flour you need. And the more flour you add, the more out of balance your dough becomes, and then you have to backtrack and add a little more of everything again. Also, I think it's true to say that, the more flour you add, the tougher the dough – and your gnocchi – will be. So, use a fine floury potato – 'balls of flour' as our Irish mammies used to call them – and your gnocchi will have a fine start in life. The quantity of flour given is a minimum amount – it should be safe to add that much in one go.

FOR FOUR:

1kg tomatoes
6 cloves garlic
1 sprig rosemary
1 sprig thyme
olive oil, to cover

600g floury potatoes
150g watercress
100g Parmesan, grated
salt and pepper, to season
120g plain white flour

300mls cream
small bunch wild garlic,
chopped

To make the tomato sauce, chop the tomatoes coarsely and put them in an oven tray with the garlic and herb sprigs, and add a coating of olive oil. Roast in a hot oven until the tomatoes are well coloured and broken down. Take out the rosemary and thyme sprigs, purée the tomatoes in their juices and pass the purée through a sieve to remove the skins.

Peel and steam, or boil and peel, the potatoes, according to your beliefs. Indeed, baking them in the oven and scooping out the cooked flesh is an excellent way to get the driest possible potato flesh. Either way, gently mash the cooked potato flesh, or pass it through a sieve. Chop the watercress very finely, put it in a clean cloth and squeeze out any moisture. Stir the watercress into the potato mash, add 80g of the Parmesan, and season well with salt and pepper. Add the flour and quickly work it into the potato. If the dough feels like it's not too sticky to roll out, nick off a small piece, roll it into a ball and drop it into boiling water to test. If it holds its shape firmly, without falling apart or getting gloopy on the outside, it's fine – don't add any more flour to the dough. If in

any doubt, add some flour and test again. When you've got a dough you trust, tear off a piece and use your hands to roll it into a long tubular shape about the thickness of your finger (or slightly thicker if you've got very elegant hands), and cut off pieces 2–3cm long. Drop the gnocchi into a large pot of boiling water, but don't overcrowd them – do a second batch separately if necessary.

While the gnocchi are cooking, put four tablespoons of the tomato sauce in a wide pan, add the cream, bring it to a boil and keep it at a very low simmer. The gnocchi are done when they float to the top. Remove the cooked gnocchi with a slotted spoon. If you are cooking two or more batches of the gnocchi, drop the cooked ones into the sauce to wait for the final batch. Then spoon the gnocchi on to plates or dishes just wide enough to hold them without crowding and pour over enough sauce to cover the surface of the plate. Scatter the chopped garlic leaves and the remaining Parmesan liberally over the gnocchi and finish the dish briefly under a hot grill, or in a hot fan oven.

Watercress, pear and walnut salad with blue cheese

Without the blue cheese, this is essentially a very simple, refreshing salad with clean flavours, and that is how I would use it most often – usually as a garnish for rich starters or as a salad with dinner at home. The cheese adds a sharp edge to the salad, and dresses it up enough to be a starter in its own right. I use mature Cashel blue here, though other semi-soft blues like Gorgonzola would be lovely too.

FOR FOUR:

200g watercress
60g walnut halves
60g mature blue cheese
1 pear
1 tablespoon walnut oil
3 tablespoons olive oil
juice of half a lemon

Pick over the watercress, discarding any less than perfect leaves and very thick stalks. Tear it into fairly big pieces – this won't be necessary if you bought the cress in prepared portions in a supermarket. Lightly toast the walnut halves. Break the cheese into a rough, large crumble. Slice the pear into thin wedges, then put everything in a bowl. Shake or whisk the oils and lemon juice together, add them to the bowl and toss the mixture gently. Now divide the salad on to plates, making sure each gets a nice proportion of cress to the other stuff.

A basic stock

A basic stock

Not all dishes need a stock. Indeed, as a younger cook I was interested only in the flavours of the main ingredients of dishes and almost never used stocks. If I felt a dish needed some complexity I put more ingredients in, spices, herbs, oils and so on. What I've come to like about using stock is the layering of flavours that can be achieved. The stock holds a balanced collection of flavours, as one, in the background as a support to the upfront primary flavours of the dish, given by the main ingredients. Think of stock as the bass tone, the element which holds the mood while the main ingredients amuse and entertain. This is important in dishes like risotto, soups and stews.

The title to this recipe doesn't lie. This is the basic model. The ingredients given here will make an acceptable, multi-purpose stock, and they are usually all present in the stocks we use in Paradiso. However, on any given day, it is likely that there will be a few extra seasonal twists. While I don't subscribe to the practice of throwing every spare piece of vegetable matter into the stockpot and boiling overnight, I do use appropriate pieces of cut-offs, leaves and stems of seasonal vegetables. In spring, for example, the asparagus stems are either added to the stockpot, or the water the asparagus is cooked in is also used to cook broad beans, green beans and spinach, and then reduced to a fraction of its volume and added to the stock; or it is used as the starting water for a stock. In winter, I prefer to use celeriac instead of celery, as it has the essential flavour of celery with an earthy tone which is very welcome in winter dishes. Other roots can be used too, though parsnips will add a sweetness you may want to make allowance for. I love tomatoes in a stock for their lovely sweet but sharp nature, but they will colour the stock, so use them only if a slightly orange tint doesn't matter. Most vegetables in their season will contribute a little something to stock, with some exceptions, such as aubergines. Bitter greens and cabbages will dominate a stock too easily, and if you do want to use them, they should only be cooked very briefly.

Herbs play a vital role in deciding the tone of the stock. As well as the basic thyme and parsley, which I would think of as staple winter herbs and use in greater amounts then, a stock in spring will often have fennel and dill herb because I like their airy, heady tone, and in later spring a little of the summer herbs. Basil and, to a lesser extent, oregano speak of the summer and should be used abundantly through the season. Tarragon and sage are powerful but deep herbs that should be used in small doses. I never use rosemary in stock because I feel it is too aromatic and overpowering, but I concede that may be a personal thing, and it's not that I don't love rosemary.

Finally, keep a very good stock powder, or bouillon, handy. I don't like it on its own, but sometimes, if a stock is lacking in depth and dimensions, if you don't have enough ingredients or herbs, add a careful pinch of a very high-quality stock powder and boil the stock for one more minute. The Swiss brand, Marigold, is excellent.

3 litres water
3 onions
8 cloves garlic
4 sticks celery
3 carrots
1 sprig thyme
1 bunch parsley
1 teaspoon peppercorns
1 teaspoons salt

To make the stock, bring the water to a boil in a large pot and drop in the rest of the ingredients. Bring it back to a boil and simmer for thirty minutes. Take the pot off the heat and leave it to rest for thirty minutes more, then drain the stock through a fine sieve to remove all the solids.

Vegetables, by and large, give up their flavour easily and long cooking can cause some to become bitter and old-tasting. A half-hour's simmering and a further half hour resting is enough to draw out the flavour of vegetables, herbs and spices. If you feel you need the stock to be stronger or more intense, you can simmer it again to reduce the volume after discarding the solids. Vegetable stocks need to be fresh, and to somehow retain something of the fresh qualities of the ingredients in them. Don't make stock from vegetables that would otherwise be destined for the compost; your stock, like everything else you cook, will taste of what you make it from.

Acknowledgements

Thanks to John Foley of Bite for the design, Jörg Köster for photography, and everyone at Atrium who was involved in getting the book onto the shelves.

The book is dedicated to the people who produce the food that we cook with: the heroic vegetable growers everywhere, but especially Ultan Walsh grows much of the food that inspires me, both in Café Paradiso and in these recipes; also the amazing cheesemakers of the burgeoning industry in Ireland, especially those who make the cheeses I use most in this book – Bill Hogan's Gabriel, Wolfgang and Agnes Schliebitz' Knockalara, Dick Willem's Coolea, Rochus and Rose's Mature Oisin.

I am, of course, hugely grateful to my wife, Bridget, who supports my writing in the best way possible – by making it seem that the inevitable absentmindedness and general uselessness induced by days of writing (and non-writing) have had no adverse effect on either home life or the smooth running of Café Paradiso.

Index